Clever with Rice

HOME COOKING

© 1994 Time-Life Books B.V.
First published jointly by Time-Life Books B.V. and
Geddes & Grosset Ltd.

Material in this book was first published as part of the series
HEALTHY HOME COOKING.

ISBN 0 7054 2025 6

Printed in Italy.

Clever with Rice

BY
THE EDITORS OF TIME-LIFE BOOKS

TIME-LIFE BOOKS/GEDDES & GROSSET

Contents

Introduction

Rice was first cultivated in China around 5000 years ago. Since then it has become the staple diet of much of Asia, South America and even Mediterranean Europe. It is grown not only in tropical conditions but also in temperate areas such as Italy and Spain. It is also grown in North America particularly in South Carolina.

Rice is a food which has inspired lots of culinary ingenuity: subtle variations in technique give strikingly different results even with similar added ingredients. To achieve the fluffy separate grains typical of a pilaff, rice is heated in fat, them simmered undisturbed, as gently as possible, in precisely the amount of liquid it can absorb without overcooking. For a risotto (page 16) the stickiness of round grain rice is exploited by cooking slowly and stirring—and the creaminess of the end result is intensified with grated cheese. Once rice has been boiled or steamed it can be used as a meat stuffing (page 13) or fried, fashioned into cakes and grilled (page 44) or used in salads (48).

The Key to Better Eating

Home Cooking addresses the concerns of today's weight-conscious, health-minded cooks with recipes that take into account guidelines set by nutritionists. The secret of eating well, of course, has to do with maintaining a balance of foods in the diet. The recipes thus should be used thoughtfully, in the context of a day's eating. To make the choice easier, an analysis is given of nutrients in a single serving. The counts for calories, protein, cholesterol, total fat, saturated fat, and sodium are approximate.

Interpreting the chart

The chart below gives dietary guidelines for healthy men, women and children. Recommended figures vary from country to country, but the principles are the same everywhere. In the UK, the average daily amounts of calories and protein are from a report by the UK Department of Health and Social Security; the maximum advisable daily intake of fat is based on guidelines given by the National Advisory Committee on Nutrition Education (NACNE); those for cholesterol and sodium are based on upper limits suggested by the World Health Organization.

The volumes in the Home Cooking series do not purport to be diet books, nor do they focus on health foods. Rather, they express a common-sense approach to cooking that uses salt, sugar, cream, butter and oil in moderation, while employing other ingredients that also provide flavour and satisfaction. The portions themselves are modest in size.

The recipes make few unusual demands. Naturally they call for fresh ingredients, offering substitutes when these are unavailable. (The substitute is not calculated in the nutrient analysis, however.) Most of the ingredients can be found in any well-stocked supermarket.

Heavy-bottomed pots and pans are recommended to guard against burning whenever a small amount of oil is used and where there is danger of the food adhering to the hot surface, but non-stick pans can be utilized as well. Both safflower oil and virgin olive oil are favoured for sautéing. Safflower oil was chosen because it is the most highly polyunsaturated vegetable fat available in supermarkets, and polyunsaturated fats reduce blood cholesterol; if unobtainable, use sunflower oil, also high in polyunsaturated fats. Virgin olive oil is used because it has a fine fruity flavour lacking in the lesser grade known as 'pure'. In addition, it is—like all olive oil—high in monounsaturated fats, which are thought not to increase blood cholesterol. When virgin olive oil is unavailable, or when its flavour is not essential to the success of the dish, 'pure' may be used.

About cooking times

To help planning, time is taken into account in the recipes. While recognizing that everyone cooks at a different speed and that stoves and ovens differ, approximate 'working' and 'total' times are provided. Working time stands for the minutes actively spent on preparation; total time includes unattended cooking time, as well as time devoted to marinating, steeping or soaking ingredients. Since the recipes emphasize fresh foods, they may take a bit longer to prepare than 'quick and easy' dishes that call for canned or packaged products, but the difference in flavour, and often in nutrition, should compensate for the little extra time involved.

Recommended Dietary Guidelines

Average Daily Intake		Calories	Protein	Maximum Daily Intake Cholesterol	Total fat	Saturated fat	Sodium
			grams	milligrams	grams	grams	milligrams
Females	7-8	1900	47	300	80	32	2000*
	9-11	2050	51	300	77	35	2000
	12-17	2150	53	300	81	36	2000
	18-54	2150	54	300	81	36	2000
	55-74	1900	47	300	72	32	2000
Males	7-8	1980	49	300	80	33	2000
	9-11	2280	57	300	77	38	2000
	12-14	2640	66	300	99	44	2000
	15-17	2880	72	300	108	48	2000
	18-34	2900	72	300	109	48	2000
	35-64	2750	69	300	104	35	2000
	65-74	2400	60	300	91	40	2000

* (or 5 g salt)

Quail Stuffed with Wild Mushrooms and Rice

Serves 4

Working time: about 45 minutes

Total time: about 1 hour

Calories 690, Protein 50g, Cholesterol 115mg, Total fat 26g, Saturated fat 8g, Sodium 585mg

8	quail (about1kg/2lb)
175 g/6 oz	long-grain white rice
60 cl/1 pint	unsalted chicken stock
³/₄ tsp	salt
30 g/1 oz	unsalted butter
30 g/1 oz	ceps or other dried mushrooms, soaked in cold water for 20 minutes, then finely chopped, the soaking liquid reserved
1	stick celery, finely chopped
1	onion, finely chopped
1 tbsp	fresh thyme, or ³/₄ tsp dried thyme freshly ground blackpepper
1 ¹/₄tsp	safflower oil
1	shallot finely chopped
125g/4 oz	small or pickling onions, blanched for 30 seconds in boiling water, drained and peeled
12.5 cl/4 fl oz	Maderia
1 tbsp	cornflour, mixed with 1 tbsp water

Preheat the oven to 170°C (325°F or Mark 3). Combine the rice, ¹/₂ litre (16 fl oz) of the stock and ¹/₄ teaspoon the salt in a fireproof casserole over medium-high heat. Bring the liquid to a simmer, then cover the casserole tightly and put it in the oven. Cook until all the liquid has been absorbed and the rice is tender—about 25 minutes—and let it stand, covered, for 10 minutes.

While the rice is cooking, melt half of the butter in a heavy frying pan over low heat. Add the mushrooms, celery, onion and half of the thyme. Cook, stirring, until the celery is tender—about 5 minutes. Remove the pan from the heat.

When the rice is ready, stir the vegetable mixture into it and set it aside uncovered. Raise the oven temperature to 220°C (425°F or Mark 7).

To prepare the quail, rinse out their cavities with cold water and pat them dry. Sprinkle the birds with ¹/₄ teaspoon of the salt and some pepper. Stuff the quail with the rice mixture, resenving the excess stuffing for an accompaniment. Spread ¹/₄ teaspoon of the oil over the bottom of a fireproof casserole large enough to hold the birds in a single layer. Set the quail breast side up in the casserole and roast them until their breasts feel firm but springy to the touch—l5 to 17 minutes.

Meanwhile, start the sauce Heat the remaining oil in a heavy-bottomed saucepan over low heat Add the shallot and sauté it for 2 minutes. Stir in the small onions, Madeira, 12.5 cl (4 fl oz) of the reserved mushroom soaking liquid, the remaining stock and the rest of the thyme. Cover tightly and simmer the mixture until the small onions are translucent—about 10 minutes.

When the quail are ready, transfer them to a warmed serving platter and pour the excess fat from the casserole. Put the reserved stuffing in a smal baking dish, and cover it with foil. Turn off the oven and place the rice mixture in the oven to heat it through.

Place the casserole over low heat and deglaze it with some of the liquid from the saucepan. Return the mixture to the saucepan. Push the onions to one side, whisk in the cornflour and water, and simmer for 2 minutes. Finish the sauce by adding the remaining salt, some pepper and the remaining butter to the saucepan. If the sauce is too thick, thin it with 2 tablespoons of the mushroom-soaking liquid. Pass the sauce separately.

Rice Congee

Serves 8

Working time: about 30 minutes

Total time: about 1 hour

Calories 165, Protein 10g, Cholesterol 20mg, Total fat 1g,
Saturated fat 0g, Sodium 130mg

135 g/4½ oz	*long-grain rice*
7 litre/13/4 pints	*unsalted brown or chicken stock*
7 tbsp	*safflower oil*
6	*garlic cloves, finely chopped*
60 g/2 oz	*fresh ginger root, julienned*
125 g/4 oz	*beansprouts*
45 g/1½ oz	*fresh coriander leaves*
1	*lime, cut into 16 wedges*
2 tbsp	*sugar*
1 tsp	*fish sauce or low-sodium soy sauce*
1 tsp	*salt*
	freshly ground black pepper
250 g/8 oz	*beef fllet, trimmed of fat and cut into thin strips*
3	*spring onions, trimmed and cut into 1 cm (½ inch) lengths*

Put the rice, stock and 1 litre (13/4 pints) of water into a large saucepan; bring the liquid to the boil. Stir the mixture, then reduce the heat to medium, and simmer. While the rice is cooking, heat the safflower oil in a small frying pan over medium-low heat. Add the garlic and cook it, stirring often, until it is crisp and brown— 4 to 5 minutes. Transfer the garlic to a paper towel and let it drain. Put the garlic, ginger, bean sprouts, coriander and lime wedges into small serving bowls, and set them aside.

About 5 minutes before serving, stir the sugar, fish sauce or soy sauce, salt and some pepper into the hot soup. Add the beef strips and spring onions, and bring the liquid to the boil. Reduce the heat to medium and simmer the soup until the beef is just cooked— about 3 minutes.

Ladle the soup into individual bowls. Pass the garnishes separately inviting the diners to season their own soup with them.

Lamb and Orange Pilaff

Serves 4
Working time about 30 minutes
Total time about 1 hour and 25 minutes
Calories 385, Protein 16g, Cholesterol 55mg, Total fat 8g,
Saturated fat 3g, Sodium 205mg

350 g/l2 oz *lean lamb (from the leg or loin), trimmed*
of fat and finely diced
1 tsp *safflower oil*
1 *onion, chopped*
1 *large leek, trimmed, washed and sliced*
200 g/7 oz *long-grain brown rice*
45 cl/³/₄ pint *unsalted brown or chicken stock*
1 tsp *chopped fresh rosemary, or ¹/₂ tsp dried*
rosemary
¹/₄ tsp *salt*
freshly ground black pepper
1 *orange, rind grated and flesh cut into*
segments
2 *carrots, peeled*
125 g/4 oz *courgettes, trimmed*
30 g/1 oz *raisins*
Preheat the oven to 180 C (350 F or Mark 4).

Heat the oil in a fireproof casserole over high heat. Add the lamb and sear it quickly on all sides. Stir in the onion, leek and rice and cook them for 1 minute. Add the stock, rosemary, salt, pepper and orange rind. Bring the mixture to the boil, then cover the casserole, transfer it to the oven and bake the pilaff until the rice is almost tender and the liquid virtually absorbed— about 40 minutes.

Using a potato peeler, shred the carrots and courgettes into long strips. Reserve a few carrot strips for garnish and stir the remainder into the lamb mixture along with the courgette strips and the raisins. Return the casserole to the oven and cook, covered, until the rice and carrots are tender—about 20 minutes. Stir in the orange segments and garnish with the reserved carrot ribbons just before serving.

11

Lamb and Wild Rice Soup

Serves 6

Working time: about 50 minutes

Total time: about 2 hours

Calories 375 Protein 19g, Cholesterol 1mg, Total fat 13g,
Saturated fat 6g, Sodium 275mg

1 tbsp	safflower oil
2	lamb shoulder joints, knuckle end (about 1 kg/2 lb, trimmed of fat)
750 g/1¹/₂ lb	onions, coarsely chopped
³/₄ litre/16 fl oz	dry white wine
400 g/14 oz	canned tomatoes, drained and chopped
³/₄ litre/1¹/₄ pints	unsalted chicken or veal stock
1	carrot, sliced into 5 mm (¹/₄ inch) thick rounds
8	garlic cloves, chopped
1	stick celery, chopped
	freshly ground black pepper
¹/₂ tsp	salt
1¹/₂ tbsp	fresh rosemary, or 1 tsp dried rosemary
160 g/5¹/₂ oz	wild rice

Heat the oil in a large, heavy frying pan over medium-high heat. Saute the lamb joints in the pan until they are dark brown all over—about 15 minutes. Transfer the browned lamb joints to a stockpot or large, heavy-bottomed saucepan.

Reduce the heat under the frying pan to medium. Add the onions and cook them, stirring frequently, until they are lightly browned—10 to 15 minutes.

Add the onions to the pot. Return the pan to the heat and immediately pour in the wine. With a wooden spoon, scrape up the caramelized pan juices from the bottom, stirring well to dissolve them. Add the tomatoes and boil the mixture until it is reduced by half—about 5 minutes. Pour the reduced liquid into the pot, then add the stock, 2.5 litres (4 pints) of water, the carrot, garlic, celery and some pepper.

Place the pot over medium heat and bring the mixture to a strong simmer, skimming off any foam that rises to the surface. Stir in the salt and rosemary. Reduce the heat and gently simmer the soup until the lamb is tender—1¹/₂ to 2 hours.

After the meat has cooked for 1 hour, put the rice into a saucepan with ¹/₄ litre (8 fl oz) of water and bring the liquid to a simmer over medium heat. Reduce the heat to low and cook the rice slowly until all of the water is absorbed—about 15 minutes. Set the rice aside.

Transfer the lamb joints to a clean work surface. When they are cool enough to handle, remove the meat from the bones. Cut the meat into small pieces; discard the bones. Return the meat to the pot. Add the partially cooked rice and simmer the soup until the rice is tender—about 20 minutes. Serve the soup hot.

Stuffed Vine Leaves

Serves 6
Working (and total) time: about 1 hour

Calories 190, Protein 16g, Cholesterol 35mg, Total fat 8g,
Saturated fat 3g, Sodium 50mg

250 g/8 oz	lean lamb (from the leg or loin), trimmed of fat and minced
60 g/2 oz	brown rice
30	fresh vine leaves, or preserved vine leaves rinsed under cold running water
1	small onion, finely chopped
30 g/1 oz	pine-nuts
30g/1 oz	currants
1 tsp	ground cinnamon
1 tsp	ground allspice
2¹/₂ tbsp	fresh lemon juice
	freshly ground black pepper
1	egg white, lightly beaten
6	garlic cloves, thinly sliced
30 cl/¹/₂ pint	puréed tomatoes
1 tsp	soft brown sugar
6 tbsp	plain low-fat yogurt, for garnish

Put the rice in a bowl with 20 cl (7 fl oz) of boiling water. Cover the bowl loosely and microwave on high for 5 minutes. Reduce the power to medium and cook for 5 minutes more. Let the rice stand for 5 minutes, then drain off any liquid and leave it to cool.

If you are using fresh vine leaves, put them in a bowl and cover them with water. Microwave on high until the water boils—about 5 minutes. Leave to stand for 10 minutes, drain and trim off the stalks.

Mix the lamb, rice, onion, pine-nuts, currants, cinnamon, allspice, 1 teaspoon of the lemon juice and some pepper together in a bowl. Mix in the egg white.

Lay a vine leaf, vein side up, on the work surface. Place a heaped teaspoon of the filling near the base of the leaf and fold the sides towards the centre. Roll up the leaf into a cigar shape. Stuff the other leaves in the same way. Place them seam side down in a baking dish and tuck the slivers of garlic between them.

Mix together the tomatoes, the remaining lemon juice, the sugar and some pepper and pour the mixture over the leaves. Cover with plastic film, leaving a corner open. Microwave on high for 10 minutes. Reduce the power to medium and cook for another 15 minutes. Allow the stuffed vine leaves to stand for 5 minutes, then serve them with the yogurt.

Shoulder Stuffed with Wild Rice and Spinach

Serves 12
Working time about I hour
Total time- about 4 hours

Calories 225, Protein 22 g, Cholesterol 75 mg, Total fat 13 g, Saturated fat 5 g, Sodium 140 mg

1. 5 kg/3 lb	shoulder of lamb, boned and trimmed
60 g/2 oz	wild rice
2 tsp	virgin olive oil
4	shallots, coarsely chopped
175 g/6 oz	celenac, grated
175 g/6 oz	fresh spinach, washed, stems removed
¹/₂ tsp	finely grated nutmeg
³/₄ tsp	salt
	freshly ground black pepper
30cl/¹/₂ pint	unsalted chicken stock
1 tsp	cornflour

To make the stuffing, wash the wild rice and put it into a large saucepan in twice its volume of water. Bring the water to the boil, cover the pan and simmer until the husks have split and the rice is soft—50 minutes to 1 hour. Drain the rice and allow it to cool. Heat the oil in a frying pan, add the shallots and cook them over very low heat until they are soft but not brown. Add the celeriac and continue cooking until it begins to look transparent—about 3 minutes—then add the spinach and cook for about 1 minute, until it wilts. Blend this mixture very briefly in a food processor to make a rough-textured puree; do not over process. Mix the puree with the wild rice, and season with the nutmeg, ¹/₂ teaspoon of the salt and some black pepper.

Preheat the oven to 230°C (450°F or Mark 8). Stuff and tie the shoulder into a melon shape. Put the lamb in a roasting pan and season the outside with the remaining salt and pepper. Roast the lamb in the oven until it is well browned—10 to 15 minutes-then reduce the oven temperature to 200°C (400°F or Mark 6) and cook for a further 1¹/₄ to 1¹/₂ hours for medium-rare to medium meat. Transfer the lamb to a carving board and allow it to rest in a warm place for 15 minutes.

While the meat is resting, make the gravy. Skim off any fat from the roasting juices and transfer the pan to the stove top. Add the stockand boil it over high heat, stirring to loosen any sediment from the bottom of the pan. Mix the cornflour with 1 tablespoon of water and add it to the pan, stirring constantly until the gravy thickens- 2 to 3 minutes. Season with black pepper. Cut off the string and carve the lamb into wedges. Serve the gravy separately.

Caucasian Lamb Kebabs with Fruity Pilaff

Serves 6

Working time: about 1 hour and 15 minutes

Total time: about 25 hours (includes marinating)

Calories 390, Protein 29g, Cholesterol 65mg, Total fat 12g, Saturated fat 4g, Sodium 150mg

2 tsp	safflower oil
1	small onion, finely chopped
400 g/14 oz	red-skinned plums or damsons, stoned and chopped
1 tbsp	red wine vinegar
1 tbsp	clear honey
1 tsp	ground cinnamon
1/4 tsp	ground allspice
	freshly ground black pepper
600 g/1 1/4 lb	lean loin of lamb, trimmed of fat and cut into 4 cm (1 1/2 inch cubes)
1 tbsp	chopped fresh basil
15 cl/1/4 pint	thick Greek yogurt

Fruity pilaf

150g/5 oz	long-grain rice
60 g/2 oz	large black raisins
60g/2 oz	dried pears, chopped
60 g/2 oz	dried apricots, chopped
12 5cl/4 fl oz	unsweetened white grape or apple juice
1 tsp	safflower oil
1/4 tsp	salt
1/4 tsp	powdered saffron
1	cinnamon stick
1 tsp	clear honey
1	fresh peach or nectarine, stoned and diced
15 g/1/2 oz	skinned almonds, toasted
7g/1/4 oz	mint, chopped

Heat the oil in a heavy frying pan, add the onion and cook it over medium heat for 5 minutes, until is soft. Add the plums, vinegar, honey, cinnamon, allspice and some black pepper, and simmer the plums until they are very soft—about 20 minutes. Purée the contents of the pan in a food processor or blender.

Place the lamb cubes in a shallow dish. Reserve 6 tablespoons of the plum purée; stir the chopped basil into the remaining purée and pour it over the lamb, turning the cubes of meat to coat them evenly. Cover the lamb loosely and place it in the refrigerator to marinate for about 24 hours.

Two hours before cooking the dish, rinse the rice, then pour 30 cl (1/2 pint) of cold water over it and leave it to soak. Remove the lamb from the refrigerator to allow it to reach room temperature. At the same time, place the raisins, dried pears and dried apricots in a bowl and pour in the grape juice.

When you are ready to cook the rice, drain it and place it in a large saucepan with an equal volume of cold water. Add the oil, salt and saffron, and bring the liquid to the boil. Stir the rice, reduce the heat, then simmer the rice gently, tightly covered, for about 20 minutes, or until the grains have absorbed all the liquid; do not stir the rice while it is cooking.

Meanwhile, transfer the dried fruit and grape juice to a non-reactive saucepan. Add the cinnamon stick and the honey, cover the pan and simmer the dried fruit until it is soft—about 10 minutes. Remove the lid and reduce the liquid until only a small amount of coating syrup remains. Discard the cinnamon stick.

Stir the cooked dried fruit and its syrup into the rice, together with the diced peach. Allow the rice to cool a little, then stir in the toasted almonds and the chopped mint. Cover the saucepan loosely and set it aside while you cook the lamb.

Lightly oil six long skewers. Thread the lamb cubes on to the skewers, reserving any excess marinade. Oil the rack lightly and cook the kebabs over medium-hot coals for about 15 minutes, turning them frequently and occasionally basting them with any remaining marinade. Rest the cooked kebabs on a warmed serving platter for 5 minutes. Meanwhile, place the yogurt in a serving bowl and gently drop the reserved plum purée on to the surface.

To serve, spoon some fruit pilaff on to a plate. Arrange the lamb cubes from one skewer on top of the pilaff and dribble some of the yogurt over the meat.

Editor's Note: Pilaf is traditionally served warm, rather than hot or cold. It may be prepared In advance and gently reheated in a shallow foil tray set over the barbecue rack, provided it is stirred frequently.

To toast almonds, place them on a baking sheet under the grill until they are golden, turn or shake them constantly while they are toasting.

Rolled Vine Leaves

Serves 8
Working time: about 45 minutes
Total time: about 2 hours and 30 minutes
Calories 110, Protein 4g, Cholesterol 20mg, Total fat 5g,
Saturated fat 2g, Sodium 65mg

125 g/4 oz	*lean minced lamb*
1	*onion, chopped*
2	*garlic cloves, chopped*
90 g/3 oz	*brown rice*
2 tbsp	*chopped fresh mint*
2 tbsp	*chopped parsley*
1 tbsp	*tomato paste*
2	*tomatoes, skinned, seeded (page 10) and chopped*
	freshly ground black pepper
125 g/4 oz	*fresh vine leaves, blanched for 1 minute in boiling water, rinsed and drained well*
1 tbsp	*virgin olive oil*
1	*lemon, juice only*
	lemon wedges, for garnish

In a non-stick or heavy cast-iron frying pan, cook the minced lamb over low heat until the meat begins to release its juices. Increase the heat to medium and continue to fry the lamb until it has browned. Place a colander over a bowl and transfer the lamb and its juices to the colander to drain. Return 1 tablespoon of the meat juices to the pan and saute the onion and the garlic in these juices over low heat, until soft—about 10 minutes. Discard the remaining meat juices.

Return the drained lamb to the frying pan and stir in the brown rice, mint, parsley, tomato paste, tomatoes and some pepper Add 20 cl (7 fl oz) of water, and bring the mixture to the boil. Cover the pan and cook the stuffing for 10 minutes, then set it aside for a few minutes to cool slightly.

Preheat the oven to 180°C (3 50°F or Mark 4). Lay the vine leaves out flat on the work surface. Place a spoonful of stuffing on the centre of each leaf. Fold the stem end up over the stuffing, fold both sides towards the middle, then roll into a small parcel. Take care not to wrap the parcels too tightly: the rice needs room to expand as it cooks.

Lay any spare or damaged vine leaves in the base of a heavy casserole. Set the stuffed parcels in the casserole, packing them in tightly to keep them from unrolling. Pour the oil, lemon juice and 45 cl (³/₄ pint) of water over the rolls.

Cover the casserole and cook the vine leaves in the oven for about 1 ¹/₄ hours, adding extra water if the liquid in the casserole evaporates. Leave the parcels to cool in the casserole Serve them cold, garnished with lemon wedges.

Editor's Note: Preserved vine leaves may be used if fresh leaves are not available. Wash them in cold water to rid them of excess salt, then drain them thoroughly on a folded tea towel. They do not require blanching

15

Pork Risotto

Serves 4
Working time: about 25 minutes
Total time about 40 minutes
Calories 460, Protein 24g, Cholesterol 55mg, Total fat
12g, Saturated fat 4g, Sodium 100mg

350 g/12 oz	*pork fillet, trimmed of fat and cut into small cubes*
1 tbsp	*virgin olive oil*
1	*garlic clove, crushed*
125 g/4 oz	*button mushrooms, rouohly chopped*
¹/₂ tsp	*chopped fresh sage*
250 g/8 oz	*Italian round-grainrice*
¹/₂ tsp	*salt*
	freshly ground black pepper
30 cl/¹/₂ pint	*dry white wine*
125 g/4 oz	*shelled peas, blanched in boiling water, or frozen peas*
1 tbsp	*freshly grated Parmesan cheese*
3tbsp	*flat-leafparsley, torn into small pieces*

Heat the olive oil in a heavy-bottomed saucepan over medium heat and brown the cubes of meat. Stir in the onion and continue cooking until the onion begins to turn golden at the edges. Add the garlic, mushrooms and sage. When the mushrooms are wilting, increase the heat, add the rice, salt and some pepper, and stir for a couple of minutes.

Mix the white wine with an equal amount of water and pour half of the liquid into the saucepan. Reduce the heat and stir while bringing the liquid to a gentle simmer. Stir the mixture frequently as the liquid is absorbed—5 to 10 minutes.

Pour in the rest of the liquid and the peas, bring back to a simmer and stir. Cover the pan and leave to cook very slowly, stirring from time to time until the mixture is creamy but not mushy—10 to 15 minutes. Just before serving, stir in the cheese and parsley.

Pork and Clam Salad

Serves 6 as a main course

Working time: about 1 hour and 30 minutes

Total time: about 3 hours and 15 minutes
(includes chilling)

Calories 425, Protein 27g, Cholesterol 75mg, Total fat 9g,
Saturated fat 2g, Sodium 290mg

500g/1 lb	boneless pork loin, trimmed of fat and cut into 1 cm (¹/₂ inch) cubes
¹/₄ litre/8 fl oz	dry white wine
2 tbsp	fresh lemon juice
¹/₂ tsp	salt
	freshly ground black pepper
¹/₄ tsp	cayenne pepper
2 tbsp	chopped fresh coriander
4	garlic cloves, finely chopped
2 tbsp	virgin olive oil
1	shallot, finely chopped
36	small hard-shell clams, scrubbed
1	small red onion, thinly sliced
1	small sweet red pepper, seeded, deribbed and cut into short, thin strips
1	small sweet green pepper, seeded, deribbed and cut into short, thin strips
4	ripe tomatoes, skinned, seeded and julienned
275g/ 9 oz	long-grain rice
¹/₂ litre/16 fl oz	unsalted chickenstock
1	bunch watercress, trimmed, washed and dried

Combine the pork, wine, 1 tablespoon of the lemon juice, the salt, some black pepper, the cayenne pepper, 1 tablespoon of the coriander and half of the chopped garlic in a non-reactive bowl Cover the bowl and refrigerate it for 2 hours

Heat 1 tablespoon of the olive oil in a large pan over medium-high heat. Add the shallot and the remaining garlic, and saute them for 1 minute Put the clams into the pan. Cover the pan and cook the clams, stirring occasionally, until they open—3 to 5 minutes. Using a slotted spoon, transfer the clams to a large bowl; discard any clams that remain closed. Strain the cooking liquid through a sieve lined with muslin, taking care not to pour into the sieve any of the accumulated sand from the pan. Discard the solids

When the clams are cool enough to handle, remove them from their shells, then dip them one at a time into the strained cooking liquid to rinse off any residual grains of sand. Transfer the rinsed clams to a bowl. Rinse out the muslin and reline the sieve with it. Strain the broth aqain and pour it over the clams.

Add to the clams the remaining lemon juice, the onion, red pepper, green pepper, tomatoes and the remaining coriander; toss the mixture well, then cover the bowl and refrigerate it.

Remove the pork loin cubes from the marinade, reserving the marinade; pat the meat dry. Heat the remaining tablespoon of oil in a heavy saucepan over medium-high heat. Add the pork cubes and sauté them until they are browned-about 5 minutes.

Add the rice, stock and reserved marinade to the pan. Bring the liquid to the boil, then reduce the heat and simmer the mixture, covered, until the rice has absorbed all the liquid and is tender-18 to 20 minutes. Remove the pork and rice from the pan and spread it in a flat dish; when it is cool, mix it with the clams and vegetables. Serve the salad on a bed of watercress.

Saffron Pork with Quail and Prawns

Serves 4

Working (and total) time: about 1 hour

Calories 380, Protein 22g, Cholesterol 75mg, Total fat 9g,
Saturated fat 3g, Sodium 100mg

250g/8 oz	*pork fillet, trimmed off fat and cut into eight pieces*
2	*quail*
1 tbsp	*virgin olive oil*
1	*red onion, finely chopped*
250 g/8 oz	*Italian round-grain rice*
1/4 tsp	*saffron powder*
2	*pinches saffron threads*
1/2 tsp	*salt*
	freshly ground black pepper
1 to 1.25 litres/ 1 1/2 to 2 pints	*unsalted chicken stock or water*
1	*green chilli pepper, seeded and finely sliced*
1	*red chilli pepper, seeded and finely sliced*
4	*large cooked prawns*

Divide each quail in two by cutting down the back and up along the breastbone. Remove any innards tha remain, wash the quail pieces and pat them dry witʰ paper towels. Rub the quail with a little of the olive oil then set aside.

Heat the remaining oil in a heavy paella pan or frying pan, and sweat the onion in it for 1 minute. Add the rice and saute for about 1 minute, then add the porkₗ and saute the whole mixture for a further 2 minutes until the pork is sealed. Add the saffron powder anc saffron threads, season with the salt and some pep per, and pour on enough chicken stock or water te cover. Bring slowly to the boil, then simmer the mix ture gently for 35 to 40 minutes, adding the remainin₉ stock or water as necessary and stirring occasionallᵧ After 30 minutes, test the rice for doneness. When i is still a little hard but nearly cooked, add the chili pep pers and prawns to heat through

While the rice mixture is cooking, grill the quail un der a hot grill until they are well browned—about 1₵ minutes. Transfer the rice and pork mixture to a larg₵ dish or individual plates and serve immediately witʰ the prawns and quail to one side.

Pilaff with Pig's Heart

Serves 6
Working tIme: about 20 minutes
Total time about 45 minutes
Calories 565, Protein 15g, Cholesterol 60mg, Total fat
15g, Saturated fat 3g, Sodium 175mg

1	pig 's heart (about 250 g/8 oz) trimmed of fat and finely diced
2 tbsp	virgin olive oil
1	onion, finely chopped
2 tbsp	pine-nuts
350 g/12 oz	long-grain rice
2 tbsp	currants
1/4 tsp	sugar
1/4 tsp	ground allspice
1/4 tsp	ground cinnamon
1/2 tsp	salt
	freshly ground black pepper
3 tbsp	finely chopped parsley

Heat the olive oil in a heavy-bottomed saucepan over medium heat and saute the diced heart for about 5 minutes. Add the onion and pine-nuts, and cook until both are beginning to colour. Add the rice and stir to coat well with oil, then stir in 3/4 litre (1/4 pints) of water and all the remaining ingredients except the parsley. Bring to the boil, reduce the heat, cover and simmer for l0 minutes.

Stir in the parsley, re-cover the pan and leave the pilaff to stand, off the heat, for 15 minutes more. Mix well and serve hot or warm.

Vine Leaves Stuffed with Pork and Rice

Serves 4

Working (and total) time: about 30 minutes

Calories 220, Protein 15g, Cholesterol 45mg, Total fat 12g, Saturated fat 4g, Sodium 250 mg

250 g/8 oz	*trimmed leg or neckend of pork, minced*
12	*large fresh vine leaves*
90 g/3 oz	*cooked brown rice*
2 tsp	*dried oregano*
1/4 tsp	*salt*
	freshly ground black pepper
1 tbsp	*fresh lemon juice*
2 tbsp	*virgin olive oil*
30 cl/1/2 pint	*unsalted chicken stock*
	lemon slices for garnish

Put the vine leaves in a bowl and cover generously with water. Microwave on high until boiling—about 5 minutes. Leave the bowl to stand for 10 minutes, then remove the vine leaves and trim away the stalks.

Mix together the minced pork, brown rice, oregano, salt and some freshly ground pepper. Place a spoonful of the pork mixture in the centre of each leaf, wrap one end of the leaf over the filling, then the two sides, and roll up into a neat parcel.

Pack the rolled vine leaves tightly in a single layer in an oval casserole dish, with their seams underneath. Pour over the lemon juice, oil and stock, which should almost cover the parcels. Cover the dish and microwave on medium for 10 minutes.

Serve the stuffed vine leaves hot or cold, garnished with the lemon slices. If serving hot, the cooking liquid may be poured over them.

Editor's Note: If you use vine leaves preserved in brine instead of fresh leaves, rinse them first under running cold water to remove the salt.

20

Nasi Goreng

Serves 6

Working time: about 25 minutes

Total time about 1 hour and 15 minutes

Calories 350, Protein 25g, Cholesterol 120mg, Total fat 12g, Saturated fat 3g, Sodium 125mg

350 g/12 oz	*pork fillet, trimmed of fat and cut into 1 cm (¹/₂ inch) cubes*
250 g/8 oz	*long-grain brown rice*
2 tbsp	*safflower oil*
1	*large onion, quartered and thinly sliced*
1	*garlic clove, chopped*
1	*green chilli pepper, seeded and chopped, plus a few thin rings for garnish*
125 g/4 oz	*boneless chicken breast, skinned and cut into 1 cm(¹/₂ inch) cubes*
¹/₂ tsp	*ground turmeric*
¹/₂ tsp	*paprika*
2 tsp	*cayenne pepper*
2 tbsp	*low-sodium soy sauce or shoyu*
1	*large tomato, skinned, seeded and cut into thin slivers*
175 g/6 oz	*peeled prawns, deveined*
Rolled omelette	
1	*egg*
1 tsp	*low-sodium soy sauce or shoyu*
1 tsp	*safflower oil*

Cook the brown rice in a large, covered, saucepan of boiling wate; until tender—about 40 minutes. Drain well, rinse under cold running water, drain well again and set aside.

Heat the oil in a large heavy frying pan. Add the sliced onion, garlic and chopped chilli pepper, and cook gently for 3 minutes, stirring frequently. Stir in the pork and chicken cubes, and cook gently for 4 minutes, stirring. Add the turmeric, paprika and cayenne pepper and mix weil, then stir in the drained rice and continue cooking the mixture for a further 4 minutes, stirring constantly. Add the soy sauce, tomato slivers and half of the prawns, and heat through for 2 to 3 minutes. Turn the mixture on to a warmed serving platter and keep warm while you make the omelette.

In a bowl, beat the egg with the soy sauce. Heat the oil in a heavy 15 to 17.5 cm (6 to 7 inch) diameter frying pan. Add the egg mixture and tilt the pan to cover the base evenly. Cook over gentle heat until the omelette is set—45 seconds to 1 minute. Loosen the omelette from the pan and turn it out on to a board, then roll up the omelette and cut it into thin slices.

Arrange the omelette slices either round the base of the rice mixture or over the top. Garnish with the reserved rings of chili pepper and the remaining prawns, and serve immediately.

Fillet with Rice and Vegetables

Serves 4
Working time: about 30 minutes
Total time: about 1 hour and 20 minutes
Calories 565, Protein 34g, Cholesterol 70mg, Total fat
15g, Saturated fat 4g, Sodium 330mg

500 g/1 lb *pork fillet, trimmed of fat and cubed*
2 tbsp *safflower oil*
1 *onion, chopped*
1 *large garlic clove, finely chopped*
500 g/1 lb *ripe tomatoes, skinned and chopped*
45 cl/³/₄ pint *pureed tomatoes*
1 tsp *mild chilli powder*
1 tbsp *Worcester sauce*
cayenne pepper
¹/₂ tsp *salt*
freshly ground black pepper
Tabasco sauce
1 *sweet green pepper, seeded, deribbed and diced*
2 *sticks celery, diced aubergine (about250 g/ 8 oz), cubed*
250 g/8 oz *courgettes, cubed*
250 g/8 oz *long-grain rice*

Heat 1 tablespoon of the oil in a large fireproof casserole over high heat. Add the pork cubes and cook until the meat is sealed—about 2 minutes—stirring all the time Stir in the onion and garlic, and cook for a further minute.

Add the chopped tomatoes, puréed tomatoes, chilli powder, Worcester sauce, a pinch of cayenne, the salt, some black pepper and a few drops of Tabasco sauce, and stir well. Cover and cook gently for 20 minutes, stirring from time to time.

Meanwhile, heat the remaining oil in a frying pan over moderate heat. Add the green pepper, celery and aubergine, and cook gently for 5 minutes, then stir in the courgettes and cook for a further 5 minutes.

Add the rice and vegetables to the meat in the casserole. Cover again and continue cooking for 10 to 15 minutes, or until the rice is tender and all the excess liquid has been absorbed. Depending on how much liquid the vegetables exude, you may need to add a little water from time to time. Fluff up the rice with a fork and serve hot.

Chicken Soup with Chilies, Cabbage and Rice

Serves 4

Working time: about 20 minutes

Total time: about 1 hour

Calories 285, Protein 20g, Cholesterol 60mg, Total fat 11g, Saturated fat 2g, Sodium 275mg

1 tbsp	*safflower oil*
750 g/1 ½ lb	*chicken thighs, skinned, fat trimmed*
1	*garlic clove, finely chopped*
3	*spring onions, trimmed and sliced into thin rounds*
½ litre/16 fl oz	*unsalted chicken stock*
1 tbsp	*fresh thyme, or ¾ tsp dried thyme freshly ground black pepper*
¼ tsp	*salt*
90 g/3 oz	*long-grain rice*
2	*large dried mild chilli pepper split lengthwise and seeded*
1	*large carrot, julienned*
175 g/6 oz	*shredded Chinese cabbage*

Heat the safflower oil in a large, heavy-bottomedsauce-pan over medium-high heat. Add the chicken thighs and saute them, turning them frequently, untilthey are evenly browned—3 to 4 minutes. Push thechicken to one side of the pan; add the garlic and spring onions and cook them for 1 minute, stirring constantly. Pour in the stock and ¾ litre (1 ¼ pints) of water. Add the thyme and some pepper, and bring the liquid to the boil. Reduce the heat to maintain a simmer and cook the mixture, partially covered, for 20 minutes. Skim any impurities from the surface and simmer the liquid for 20 minutes more.

While the stock is simmering, bring ¼ litre (8 fl oz) of water and ⅛ teaspoon of the salt to the boil in another saucepan. Add the rice and stir once, then reduce the heat and cover the pan. Simmer the rice until all of the water is absorbed—about 20 minutes.

While the rice is cooking, pour ¼ litre (8 fl oz) of boiling water over the chilies and soak for 15 minutes. Purée the chillies with their soaking liquid in a blender. (Or pulverize the soaked chillies with a mortar and pestle, gradually adding the liquid to incorporate it into the paste.)

With a slotted spoon, remove the chicken thighs from the pan and set them aside. When the chicken is cool enough to handle, remove the meat from the bones with your fingers and cut it into small pieces; discard the bones. Return the chicken pieces to the pan. Add the carrot, cabbage, rice and the remaining salt. Increase the heat to maintain a simmer and cook the soup until the carrot is tender—3 to 4 minutes. Strain the chilli purée through a fine sieve into the soup. Stir to incorporate the purée and serve the soup at once.

Spanish-Style Chicken and Saffron Rice

Serves 4

Working time: about 30 minutes

Total time: about 1 hour and 30 minutes

Calories 570, Protein 41g, Cholesterol 105mg Total fat 20g, Saturated fat 4g, Sodium 410mg

1.25 kg/2 ¹/₂ lb	chicken, skinned, cut in to serving pieces
	freshly ground black pepper
¹/₂ tsp	salt
3 tbsp	virgin olive oil
2	medium onions, thinly sliced
175 g/6 oz	long-grain brown rice
12.5cl/4 fl oz	dry white wine
¹/₈ tsp	crushed saffron threads
35 cl/12 fl oz	unsalted chicken stock
2 tbsp	mildly hot chillies
¹/₈ tsp	crushed cumin seeds
2	garlic cloves, finely chopped
2	large ripe tomatoes, skinned, seeded and chopped
1	each red and yellow sweet pepper. grilled, skinned, seeded and cut into 2 5 cm(1 inch) strips
	fresh coriander for garnish (optional)

Sprinkle the chicken pieces with pepper and ¹/₄ teaspoon of salt. In a lidded fireproof 4 litre (7 pint) casserole, heat 2 tablespoons of the olive oil over medium-high heat Sauté the chicken until golden-brown—about 4 minutes on each side—and remove to a plate.

Add the remaining tablespoon of oil to the casserole and cook the onions over medium heat until translucent—about 10 minutes. Add the brown rice and cook 2 minutes, stirring constantly to coat the grains thoroughly; pour in the white wine, bring to the boil, then reduce the heat, cover, and simmer until all the liquid has been absorbed—about 8 minutes. Add the saffron to the stock and pour over the rice. Stir in the chillies, cumin seeds, the remaining salt and the garlic. Simmer 15 minutes more and add the tomatoes and chicken, pushing them down into the rice. Cook until the juices run clear when a thigh is pierced with the tip of a sharp knife—about 25 minutes more. Garnish with the pepper strips and coriander

Greek-Style Chicken and Rice Casserole

Serves 8 as a main dish
Working time: about 30 minutes
Total time: about 1 hour

Calories 275, Protein 17g, Cholesterol 50mg, Total fat 11g, Saturated fat 3g, Sodium 245mg

2 tbsp	*safflower oil*
8	*chicken thighs, skinned*
175 g/6 oz	*long-grain rice*
1	*onion, chopped*
4	*garlic cloves, finely chopped*
¼ litre/8 fl oz	*unsalted chicken stock*
800 g/1¾ lb	*canned whoie tomatoes*
3 tbsp	*chopped fresh oregano, or 2 tsp dried oregano*
1 tbsp	*fresh thyme, or 1 tsp dried thyme*
12	*oil-cured olives, stoned and quartered, or 12 stoned black olives coarsely chopped*
30 g/1 oz	*feta cheese, rinsed and crumbled*

Heat the oil in a large, heavy fireproof casserole over medium-high heat. Add four of the thighs and cook them until they are lightly browned—about 4 minutes on each side. Remove the first four thighs and brown the other four. Set all the thighs aside.

Reduce the heat to medium and add the rice, onion, garlic and 4 tablespoons of the stock. Cook the mixture, stirring constantly, until the onion is translucent—about 4 minutes. Add the remaining stock, the tomatoes, the oregano and the thyme. Push the thighs down into the rice mixture. Bring the liquid to the boil, reduce the heat, and simmer the chicken, tightly covered, until the rice is tender—20 to 30 minutes.

Stir the olives into the chicken and rice, and serve the casserole with the feta cheese on top.

Prunes Stuffed with Wild Rice and Turkey

Makes 14 stuffed prunes

Working time: about 30 minutes

Total time: about I hour and 30 minutes

Per stuffed prune:Calories 25, Protein 2g, Cholesterol 5mg, Total fat trace, Saturated fat trace, Sodium 30mg

30 g/1 oz	*wild rice*
1/4 litre/8 fl oz	*unsalted chicken, beef or veal stock, or water*
14	*large ready-to-eatprunes*
60 g/2 oz	*smoked turkey or chicken, finely chopped*
	freshly grated nutmeg
1/4 tsp	*salt*
	freshly ground black pepper
1 tbsp	*finely cut chives*

Put the rice and stock or water into a heavy-bottomed saucepan, bring to the boil, then simmer, covered, until the husks of the rice have split—50 to 60 minutes. Drain off any remaining cooking liquid and set the rice aside to cool.

Using a sharp knife, slit open one side of each prune from end to end. Mix the turkey with the rice, season with some nutmeg, the salt and a little pepper, and stuff the prunes with this mixture. Sprinkle the chives over the stuffed prunes and serve.

Editor's Note: The prunes used in this recipe are sold for eatingstraightfrom thepacket, and do not require either presoaking or stoning. If you use ordinary dried prunes, soak them for 10 minutes 10 boiling water with a dash of Madeira and then stone them.

Duck and Wild Rice Salad with Raspberry Vinaigrette

Serves 6 as a main course at lunch
Working time: about 30 minutes
Total time: about 3 hours and 10 minutes
(includes chilling)
Calories 310, Protein 25g, Cholesterol 75mg, Total fat 12g, Saturated fat 4g, Sodium 110mg

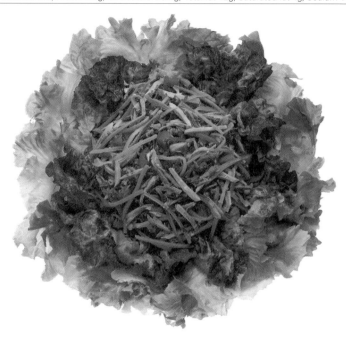

2kg/4 lb	*duck rinsed and patted dry*
5 tbsp	*raspberry vinegar*
160 g/5 ¹/₂ oz	*wild rice*
1	*garlic clove, finely chopped*
100 g/3 ¹/₂ oz	*carrot, julienned*
120 g/4 oz	*celery, julienned*
1	*large ripe tomato, skinned, seeded and*
	coarsely chopped
1 tsp	*Dijon mustard*
1 tbsp	*finely chopped shallot*
	freshly ground black pepper
3 tbsp	*unsalted chicken stock or water*
2 tsp	*safflower oil*
	small red-leaf lettuce, washed and dried
1	*small Batavian endive,washed and dried*

Trim any excess fat from around the neck of the duck. Remove any fat from the cavity. To release body fat from the duck without rendering its juices as it cooks, lightly prick the duck, taking care not to pierce the flesh below the layer of fat. Using wooden toothpicks, fasten the neck skin to the back of the duck. Sprinkle the inside of the cavity with 1 tablespoon of the vinegar. Place the duck breast side down in a microwavesafe roasting pan and cover it with grease-proof paper. Microwave the duck on medium high (70 per cent power) for 15 minutes. Drain off and discard the fat in the roasting pan. Turn the duck breast side up and cover it with fresh paper. Continue cooking the duck on medium high until the juices run clear when a thigh is pierced with the tip of a sharp knife—about 20 minutes. Drain off and discard the fat, and set the duck aside to cool.

Meanwhile, bring 60 cl (1 pint) of water to the boil in a saucepan. Pour the water into a bowl and add the wild rice and garlic. Cover the bowl and microwave the rice on medium low (30 per cent power) until it is tender—about 30 minutes. Drain the rice, transfer it to a large bowl, and refrigerate it.

Put the carrot and celery julienne into a bowl with 2 tablespoons of hot water. Cover the bowl and microwave the vegetables on high until they are tender—2 to 3 minutes. Drain the vegetables and combine them with the rice; return the mixture to the refrigerator.

When the duck is cool enough to handle, pull off its skin. Cut the meat from the duck and slice it into thin strips. Toss the strips with the rice-and-vegetable mixture. Stir in the tomato and 2 tablespoons of the remaining vinegar, and set the bowl aside.

In a small bowl, combine the mustard, shallot, some pepper, the remaining vinegar and the stock or water. Whisking vigorously, pour in the oil in a thin, steady stream; continue whisking until the mixture is well combined. Pour the vinaigrette over the duck mixture and toss it well. Chill the salad for about 2 hours to meld its flavours.

To serve the salad, arrange the lettuce and Batavian endive leaves on a serving platter and mound the salad on top of them. Serve immediately.

Chicken-Stuffed Peppers

Serves 6
Working time: about 45 minutes
Total time: about 7 hours (includes chilling)
Calories 140, Protein 9g, Cholesterol 20mg, Total fat 4g, Saturated fat 1g, Sodium 75mg

3	*small sweet red peppers, tops cut off and reserved, seeds and ribs removed*
3	*small sweet yellow peppers, tops cut off and reserved, seeds and ribs removed*
15cl/¹/₄ pint	*unsalted chicken stock*
1 tbsp	*virgin olive oil*
	Spiced chicken stuffing
¹/₂ tbsp	*virgin olive oil*
1	*onion, finely chopped*
125 g/4 oz	*long-grain rice*
2	*garlic cloves, crushed*
¹/₂ tsp	*ground cardamom*
¹/₂ tsp	*ground cumin*
250 g/8 oz	*boned chicken breast, skinned and cut into tiny cubes*
30cl/¹/₂ pint	*unsalted chicken stock*
¹/₄ tsp	*salt*
	freshly ground black pepper

First prepare the stuffing. In a large saucepan, heat the oil, then add the onion and cook gently until the onion has softened but not browned—5 to 6 minutes. Stir in the rice, garlic, cardamom and cumin. Cook for 1 to 2 minutes, then stir in the chicken pieces, stock, salt and some pepper. Bring the mixture to the boil, reduce the heat, cover the pan with a tightly fitting lid and cook very gently until the rice is tender and all of the stock has been absorbed—25 to 30 minutes.

Preheat the oven to 180°C (350°F or Mark 4).

Cook the peppers and their lids in boiling water until they soften slightly—4 to 5 minutes. Place the peppers in a large colander, refresh them under cold running water and drain them well.

Fill the peppers with the rice and chicken mixture and cover them with their lids. Stand the peppers in a deep ovenproof dish, add the chicken stock and cover the dish with a lid or with foil. Bake the peppers in the oven until they are very tender—about 1 ¹/₂ hours.

Using a slotted spoon, carefully transfer the cooked peppers to a serving dish. Pour the juices left in the baking dish into a saucepan, bring them to the boil and boil rapidly until they are reduced by half, then whisk in the olive oil. Pour this liquid over the peppers, and set them aside to cool. When the peppers have cooled, cover them with plastic film and place them in the refrigerator until they are well chilled—3 to 4 hours, or overnight—before serving.

Roulades of Plaice with Seaweed, Spinach and Rice

Serves 4

Working time: about 20 minutes

Total time: about 45 minutes

Calories 245, Protein 25g, Cholesterol 55mg, Total fat 2g, Saturated fat 1g, Sodium 665mg

500 g/1 lb	*plaice or sole fillets, cut lengthwise into 8 equal pieces*
90 g/3 oz	*rice*
30 cl/½ pint	*unsalted tomato juice*
½ tsp	*fennel seeds*
¼ tsp	*salt*
250 g/8 oz	*fresh spinach*
	white pepper
2	*sheet snori (dried roasted seaweed)*
1 tbsp	*cornflour*
¼ litre/8 fl oz	*fishstock*
2 tbsp	*mirin (sweetened Japanese rice wine) or cream sherry*
2 tbsp	*low-sodium soy sauce or shoyu*
2 tsp	*rice vinegar*
4 or 5	*drops Tabasco sauce*
2 tbsp	*chopped parsley*

To prepare the filling, combine the rice, tomato juice, fennel seeds and salt in a 1 litre (2 pint) measuring jug or glass bowl and cover it. Microwave the filling on high for 12 minutes, then set it aside, still covered.

Wash and stem the sDinach. Put the sDinach with just the water that clings to it into a 2 litre (3½ pint) baking dish. Cover the dish with plastic film and microwa,ve it on high for 3 minutes. Remove the spinach from the oven and let it cool.

Rinse the fillets under cold running water and pat them dry with paper towels. Lay the fillets side by side, with their darker sides up, on a work surface; season them with the white pepper. Spread a thin layer of the rice filling on each fillet. Cut a strip of norito fit each fillet. Lay the strips in place on the rice, then cover each strip of nori with some spinach. Roll each fillet into a roulade, rolling end to end as you would do to form a swiss roll.

Mix the cornflour with 2 tablespoons of the stock; then, in the same dish you used to cook the spinach, stir together the remaining stock, the cornflour mixture, the mirin, soy sauce, vinegar and Tabasco sauce. Microwave the mixture on high for 3 minutes; stir the resulting sauce until it is smooth. Lay the roulades in the sauce, their seam sides down; they should be close but not touching. Cover the dish and microwave it on high for 6 minutes. Let the dish stand for 3 minutes. Just before serving the roulades, spoon some of the sauce over them and garnish them with the parsley.

Mussel Risotto

Serves 6

Working (and total) time: about 45 minutes

Calories 310, Protein 20g, Cholesterol 90mg, Total fat 9g, Saturated fat 3g, Sodium 450mg

1.5kg/3 lb *mussels,scrubbed and debearded*
1 tbsp *safflower oil*
1 *onion, finely chopped*
185 g/6 ½ oz *rice*
4 tbsp *dry white wine*
8 to 10 *saffron threads, crushed (about ⅛ tsp)*
90 g/3 oz *small broccoli florets*
15 g/½ oz *unsalted butter*
60 g/2 oz *Parmesan cheese, freshly grated*
¼ tsp *white pepper*

Put the mussels in a large pan. Pour in 4 tablespoons of water, bring it to the boil, and tightly cover the pan. Steam the mussels until they open—5 to 6 minutes. With a slotted spoon, transfer the opened mussels to a bowl; discard any that remain closed. Strain the mussel cooking liquid through a fine strainer into a large measuring jug and set it aside.

Heat the oil in a fireproof casserole over medium heat. Add the onion and cook it, stirring occasionally, until it is translucent—2 to 3 minutes. Add the rice and stir to coat it with the oil. Cook for 1 minute more.

Pour in the wine and cook, stirring, until it has evaporated—about 2 minutes.

Strain into the measuring jug any liquid that has accumulated from the mussels. Add enough water to yield 35 cl (12 fl oz). Pour the liquid into the casserole and stir in the saffron. Bring the liquid to the boil, then reduce the heat to maintain a simmer. Cook the rice, stirring often, until it has absorbed most of the liquid—about 10 minutes.

Stir in ¼ litre (8 fl oz) of hot water and continue to cook the rice, stirring, until the water is absorbed. Pour in another ¼ litre (8 fl oz) of hot water; if necessary to maintain a very moist consistency, pour in an additional 12.5 cl (4 fl oz) of water. The rice is done when it is tender to the bite—25 to 30 minutes.

While the rice is cooking, remove the mussels from their shells and set the mussels aside; discard the shells. Bring 1 litre (1¾ pints) of water to the boil in a saucepan. Add the broccoli and blanch it until it is barely tender—about 2 minutes. Drain the broccoli and refresh it under cold running water.

Melt the butter in a large, heavy frying pan over medium-high heat. Add the reserved mussels and broccoli florets, and saute them until they are heated through—1 to 2 minutes. Stir the cheese and pepper into the cooked rice, then stir in the mussels and broccoli; serve at once.

Clams and Rice Yucatan-Style

Serves 4
Working time: about 30 minutes
Total time: about 1 hour

Calories 470, Protein 15g, Cholesterol 35mg, Total fat 8g,
Saturated fat 1g, Sodium 200mg

36	clams, scrubbed
3	ripe tomatoes, skinned, seeded and coarsely chopped
1	large onion, coarsely chopped
3	garlic cloves, coarsely chopped
3	fresh hot green chilli peppers, seeded and coarsely chopped
55 cl/18 fl oz	fish stock or water
2 tbsp	safflower oil
275 g/9 oz	long-grain rice
1/4 tsp	salt
	freshly ground black pepper
75 g/2 1/2 oz	shelled peas, blanched for l minute if fresh
1	lime, juice only
	several fresh coriander sprigs

Puree the tomatoes, onion, garlic, chillies and 12.5 cl (4 fl oz) of the fish stock or water in a food processor or blender. Preheat the oven to 200°C (400°F or Mark 6).

Heat the oil in a large shallow fireproof casserole over medium heat. Add the rice and saute it in the oil, stirring constantly, until it is lightly browned—3 to 4 minutes. Stir in the puréed tomato, the remaining stock or water, the salt and black pepper. Bring the mixture to a simmer, reduce the heat to medium low and cook the rice, covered, until most of the liquid has been absorbed—about 15 minutes. Stir in the peas.

Tap the clams and discard any that do not close. Arrange them on top of the rice, cover with foil and bake them until they open—about 10 minutes. Dribble the lime juice over the clams and garnish the dish with the coriander sprigs. Serve immediately.

31

Tricolour Terrine

Serves 8

Working time: about 1 hour and 30 minutes

Total time: about 13 hours (includes marinating)

Calories 275, Protein 12g, Cholesterol 35mg, Total fat 12g, Saturated fat 2g, Sodium 55mg

---

2 fresh salmon fillets, skinned and trimmed (about 400 g/14 oz)

$1/2$ tsp *caster sugar*

2 tsp *chopped fresh dill*

250g/8 oz *sushi rice*

1 tbsp *rice or white wine vinegar*

3 *sheet snori seaweed*

1 *sweet yellow pepper, skinned, seeded and deribbed, cut into 1 cm ($1/2$ inch) wide strips and patted dry*

1 *cos lettuce, ribs removed, leaves blanched, refreshed in cold water and drained thoroughly*

4 *dill sprigs, leaves only*

1 *sweet red pepper, skinned, seeded and deribbed, cut into 1 cm ($1/2$ inch) wide strips and patted dry*

12 *salad leaves, such as oakleaf lettuce and curly endive, washed and dried*

Horseradish vinaigrette

$1/2$ tbsp *rice or white wine vinegar*

3 tbsp *grape seed oil or safflower oil*

$1/4$ tsp *wasabi powder (Ja panese horseradish)*

Place the salmon on a wooden board or work surface. Combine the sugar and the chopped dill in a small bowl and rub this dry marinade all over the fish.

Sandwich the salmon fillets between two flat plates, wrap plastic film round the plates, and stand weights— such as kitchen weights or unopened tins—on top. Place the fish in the refrigerator to marinate for 12 to 24 hours. To make sure the fish becomes thoroughly permeated by the marinade, remove the plates from the refrigerator once or twice during this period, unwrap the fillets and turn them over in the marinade, then refrigerate them, well wrapped, once again.

When the fish has been marinating long enough, rinse the rice in cold water and drain it in a sieve. Put the rice in a saucepan with $1/4$ litre (8 fl oz) of water, bring it to the boil, cover the pan with a lid, and simmer

the rice over very low heat for 20 minutes. Turn off the heat and leave the rice to steam for a further IO minutes with the lid on. Remove the lid, mix in the rice vinegar and set the rice aside until it is cool— 20 to 30 minutes.

Remove the salmon from the refrigerator, pour off the liquid that has collected in the dish, and use a knife to scrape off the dry marinade. Dry the fish with paper towels, and cut it across the grain into strips about I cm ($1/2$ inch) wide.

Rub the base and sides of a $3/4$ litre (1 $1/4$ pint) terrine with wet paper towels to moisten them, and line the terrine with the nori, draping about 2 cm ($3/4$ inch) of the seaweed sheets over the sides of the dish.

Divide the rice into four equal portions. Place one quarter of the rice in the terrille, pressing it down with your fingertips to make an even base. Top the rice with the yellow pepper and follow with another layer of rice, pressing both layers.

Place half the lettuce and a sprinkling of dill on the second layer of rice. Top the leaves with the salmon strips, followed by the remaining lettuce and the dill. Pressing each layer down as you go along, cover the lettuce with the third portion of rice, top the rice with the red pepper strips and finish with a final rice layer. Place a sheet of nori on top of the terrine, and tuck down its edges over the rice.

Cover the terrine with a sheet of plastic film. Set a piece of.cardboard on the plastic film and place a weight on top of the cardboard. Put the weighted terrine in the refrigerator to set for 30 minutes. Meanwhile, combine the vinaigrette ingredients in a small bowl and mix them thoroughly with a fork.

Remove the terrine from the refrigerator and unmould it by inverting it over a platter. To serve the terrine, slice it carefully with a knife that has been dipped in water to prevent the rice from sticking. Accompany each slice with a selection of the lettuce leaves and some of the vinaigrette in a small bowl.

Editor's Note: Because the salmon in this recipe is not cooked, only the freshest fish should be used. Novi, sushi rice and wasabi powder can be purchased from Oriental grocers or health food shops. If sushi rice is unobtainable, another glutinous rice such as pudding nce may be substituted.

Salad of Monkfish and Wild Rice

Serves 8

Working time: about 25 minutes

Total time: about 2 hours

Calories 310, Protein 18g, Cholesterol 30mg, Total fat 8g, Saturated fat 1g, Sodium 300mg

500 g/l lb	*monkfish fillets*
1/4 litre/8 fl oz	*fish stock or court-bouillon*
4 tbsp	*chopped shallots*
2	*garlic cloves, finely chopped*
1 1/2 tbsp	*chopped fresh sage, or 1 1/2 tsp dried sage*
1/2 tsp	*salt*
	freshly ground black pepper
250g/8 oz	*wild rice*
1/4 litre/8 fl oz	*dry white wine*
1	*lemon, juice only*
175 g/6 oz	*shelled young broad beans, thawed if frozen*
4 tbsp	*thinly sliced sun-dried tomatoes*
250 g/8 oz	*mange-tout, strings removed, pods cut diagonally in half*
3 tbsp	*virgin olive oil*

Pour the stock or court-bouillon and 45 cl (³/4 pint) of water into a large saucepan. Add 2 tablespoons of the shallots, half of the garlic and half of the sage, 1/4 teaspoon of the salt and some pepper; bring the liquid to the boil. Stir in the rice, reduce the heat to low and partially cover the pan. Simmer the rice with the lid slightly ajar until the rice has absorbed the liquid and is tender—40 to 50 minutes.

While the rice is cooking, prepare the poaching liquid. In a large, non-reactive saute pan over medium heat, combine the wine, 12.5 cl (4 fl oz) of water, the lemon juice, the remaining shallots, the remaining garlic and sage, and the remaining salt. Grind in a generous amount of pepper.

Rinse the fillets under cold running water, then cut them into bite-sized pieces. When the poaching liquid is hot, reduce the heat to low and place the fish in the liquid. Gently poach the fish for 5 minutes until the flesh just flakes.

Transfer the fish to a plate. Let it cool slightly, then refrigerate it. Do not discard the poaching liquid.

When the rice is done, refrigerate it in a large mixing bowl. Increase the heat to high and boil the poaching liquid for 5 minutes to reduce it slightly. Add the broad beans and tomatoes, and cook them for 3 minutes. Stir in the mange-tout and cook the mixture for 1 minute more, stirring constantly; there should be just 2 or 3 tablespoons of liquid remaining.

With a slotted spoon, transfer the vegetables to the bowl with the rice. Whisk the olive oil into the reduced liquid in the pan and pour this sauce over the rice and vegetables. Toss together well. Add the fish to the bowl and gently toss the salad once more. Serve at room temperature or chilled.

34

Rice-Coated Fish Balls with Mange-Tout

Serves 4

Working (and total) time about 35 minutes

Calories 105, Protein 14g, Cholesterol 50mg, Total fat 1g, Saturated fat 0g, Sodium 60mg

45 g/1¹/₂ oz	*long-grain rice*
300 g/10 oz	*white fish fillet (such as cod, haddock or plaice), skinned*
4	*spring onions, finely sliced*
1	*garlic clove, crushed*
2.5 cm/ 1 inch	*piece fresh ginger root, grated*
1 tsp	*fresh lemon juice*
	freshly ground black pepper
90 g/3 oz	*mange-tout, topped and tailed*
4	*lemon slices, for garnish*

Cook the rice in boiling water for 5 minutes Drain it in a colander and set it aside.

In a food processor, process the fish for about 10 seconds until it begins to break down Place it in a mixing bowl with the spring onion, garlic, ginger, lemon juice and some black pepper, and mix well.

Divide the fish mixture into eight equal portions. Moisten your hands with a little water and shape each portion into a ball. Roll each ball in the parboiled rice so that the rice forms a coating

Arrange the fish balls in one layer in a steamer and place them over boiling water. Cover the pan and steam the fish balls for 7 minutes.

Just before serving, bring some water to the boil and blanch the mange-tout for 1 minute. Drain them thoroughly in a colander.

Remove the cooked fish balls from the steamer with a slotted spoon. Arrange them on individual serving plates with the mange-tout, garnish with the lemon slices, and serve hot.

Kedgeree

Serves 8

Working time: about 30 minutes

Total time: about 1 hour and 30 minutes

Calories 30, Protein 18g, Cholesterol 90mg, Total fat 3g,
Saturated fat 1g, Sodium 250mg

500 g/1 lb	*fresh haddock fillet*
125 g/4 oz	*smoked haddock fillet*
1 tbsp	*safflower oil*
1	*onion, thinly sliced*
2 tsp	*mild chilli powder*
1 tsp	*turmeric*
1 tsp	*ground ginger*
1/2 tsp	*ground coriander*
1/2 tsp	*ground cumin*
1/4 tsp	*mixed spice*
1/2 tsp	*salt*
	freshly ground black pepper
500 g/1 lb	*long-grain rice*
2	*hard-boiled eggs, quartered*

chopped fresh chives or parsley, for garnish

Put the fresh haddock into a large saucepan and add water to cover. Bring the water to a simmer and poach the fish for 5 minutes. Add the smoked haddock and continue poaching for 5 to 10 minutes or until both fish are cooked and flake easily when tested with a fork.

Drain the fish, reserving the cooking liquid. When the fish are cool enough to handle, flake them, discarding all skin and bones. Set the flaked fish aside and keep it warm.

Strain the cooking liquid and measure it; you will need 1.25 litres (2 pints); if necessary, add a little water.

Heat the oil in a large fireproof casserole or saucepan. Add the onion and cook gently, covered, for about 7 minutes or until softened. If necessary, add a few spoonfuls of the reserved cooking liquid to prevent the onion sticking and burning.

Stir in all the spices, the salt, some pepper and 2 to 3 more spoonfuls of the cooking liquid. Add the rice and stir until it is coated with the spice mixture. Add the remaining liquid and bring to the boil. Stir once, then cover and cook over very low heat for about 20 minutes or until the rice is cooked and tender and all the liquid has been absorbed.

Mussel Salad

Serves 4 as a first course

Working time: about 30 minutes

Total time: about 1 hour

Calories 175, Protein 7g, Cholesterol 25mg, Total fat 5g,
Saturated fat 1g, Sodium 125mg

90 g/3 oz	*rice*
1 tbsp	*fennel seeds*
2 tbsp	*finely chopped sweet green pepper*
4 tbsp	*finely chopped red onion*
1	*small ripe tomato, skinned, seeded and chopped*
1	*small garlic clove, finely chopped*
1 tbsp	*grated horse radish, drained*
3 tbsp	*white wine vinegar*
24	*mussels, scrubbed and debearded*
1 tbsp	*virgin olive oil*
	parsley sprigs for garnish

Put the rice, the fennel seeds and 1/4 litre (8 fl oz) of water into a small saucepan over medium-high heat. Bring the water to the boil, then reduce the heat, cover the pan, and simmer the rice until it is tender—20 to 25 minutes. Set the rice aside.

While the rice is simmering, prepare the marinade. In a non-reactive bowl, mix together the green pepper, onion, tomato, garlic, horseradish and vinegar. Set the marinade aside while you cook the mussels.

Bring 1/4 litre (8 fl oz) of water to the boil in a large pan. Add the mussels and cover the pan. Steam the mussels until they open—2 to 3 minutes. Discard any mussels that remain closed. Strain the cooking liquid through a sieve lined with doubled muslin, taking care not to pour any of the sand into the sieve. Reserve the liquid.

Using a slotted spoon, transfer the mussels to a large bowl. When the mussels are cool enough to handle, remove them from their shells, reserving one half of each shell. Dip each mussel into the reserved liquid to rinse away any residual sand. Pat the mussels dry, then add them to the marinade, and let them stand at room temperature for 30 minutes.

Stir the rice and oil into the marinated mussels. Fill each reserved mussel shell with one mussel and about 2 teaspoons of the rice-and-vegetable mixture. Arrange the stuffed shells on a platter; garnish the platter with the parsley just before serving.

Lemon Sole Roulades

Makes 24 roulades
Working time: about 35 minutes
Total time: about 50 minutes
Per roulade: Calories 40, Protein 6g, Cholesterol 20mg, Total fat 1g, Saturated fat trace, Sodium 45mg

12 *large Chinese cabbage leaves*
2 *lemon soles (about 350 g/12 oz each), cut*
into eight fillets and skinned
lemon slices, for garnish
spicy rice filling
60 g/2 oz *long-grain brown rice*
¹/₄ tsp *salt*
60 g/2 oz *button mushrooms, chopped*
2 *tomatoes, skinned, seeded and chopped*
30 g *creamed coconut*
¹/₂ tsp *curry powder*
1 tsp *grated fresh ginger root*

To prepare the filling, add the rice and salt to 17.5 cl (6 fl oz) of water. Bring to the boil in a tightly covered saucepan, then reduce the heat and simmer until the rice is tender and all of the water is absorbed—about 20 minutes. Stir in the mushrooms, tomatoes, coconut, curry powder and ginger. Mix well and set aside.

Preheat the oven to 200°C (400°F or Mark 6). Soak 24 cocktail sticks in water for about 10 minutes to pre-

vent them from scorching in the oven. Line a baking sheet with non-stick parchment paper.

Blanch the Chinese cabbage in boiling water for 15 seconds. Drain and refresh under cold running water, then drain again thoroughly. Cut each leaf lengthwise into two, removing and discarding the stem. Fold each cabbage piece to form a strip about 15 cm (6 inches) long by 2 cm (³/₄ inches) wide. Divide the rice filling into 24 portions and cover each leaf strip evenly with one portion of the filling.

Using a sharp knife, cut each sole fillet into three strips about 2 cm (³/₄ inch) wide. Place a strip of sole on each rice-topped leaf. Roll up the leaf neatly and secure with a cocktail stick.

Place the rolls on the prepared baking sheet and bake until the fish is tender and the leaves are still bright green—5 to 6 minutes.

Serve warm, garnished with the lemon slices.

Apricots and Water Chestnuts in Wild Rice

Serves 8 as a side dish
Working time: about 30 minutes
Total time: about 1 hour
Calories130, Protein 4g, Cholesterol 0mg, Total fat 0g,
Saturated fat 0g, Sodium 75mg

160 g/5¹/₂ oz	*wild rice*
125 g/4 oz	*dried apricots, cut into 1 cm(¹/₂inch) pieces*
175 g/6 oz	*fresh water chestnuts, peeled and quartered, or 250 g(8 oz)canned whole peeled water chestnuts, drained, rinsed and quartered*
2 tbsp	*chopped parsley*
	Spicy lemon dressing
2 tbsp	*fresh lemon juice*
1 tbsp	*red wine vinegar*
¹/₈ tsp	*ground ginger*
¹/₈ tsp	*cinnamon*
	ground cloves
¹/₄ tsp	*salt*
	freshly ground black pepper

Bring 1.5 litres (2¹/₂ pints) of water to the boil in a saucepan. Stir in the wild rice, reduce the heat, and simmer the rice, uncovered, until it is tender but still chewy—approximately 45 minutes.

While the rice cooks, prepare the apricots and dressing: put the apricots into a small bowl and pour in enough hot water to cover them by about 2.5 cm (1 inch). Soak the apricots for 20 minutes to soften them. Drain the apricots, reserving 4 tablespoons of their soaking liquid, and set them aside.

Pour the reserved apricot-soaking liquid into a small bowl. Add the lemon juice, vinegar, ginger, cinnamon, a pinch of cloves, the salt and some pepper; whisk the mixture vigorously until it is thoroughly combined.

When the rice finishes cooking, drain and rinse it, and transfer it to a serving bowl . Pour the dressing over the rice, then add the apricots, water chestnuts and the pa!sley; toss the ingredients well and serve the salad at room temperature.

Wild and Brown Rice Pilaff with a Mushroom Ragout

Serves 8

Working time: about 45 minutes

Total time: about 3 hours (includes soaking)

Calories 390, Protein 14g, Cholesterol 5mg, Total fat 11g,
Saturated fat 2g, Sodium 265mg

250 g/8 oz	dried flageolet beans, picked over
2	bay leaves
125 g/4 oz	wild rice
15 cm/6 inch	cinnamon stick
1 tsp	salt
300 g/l0 oz	brown basmati rice, rinsed under cold running water until the water runs clear, then soaked in 1 ¹/2 litres (2 ¹/2 pints) of water for 15 minutes
2	blades of mace
2 tsp	light brown sugar
400 g/14 oz	baby sweet corn, thickly sliced
4 tbsp	hazelnut or walnut oil
¹/2 tsp	freshly grated nutmeg
	freshly ground black pepper
	Yogurt-mushroom ragout
15 g/¹/2 oz	unsalted butter
1	small onion, finely chopped
500 g/1 lb	mixed fresh wild mushrooms, such as chanterelles, ceps, oyster or field mushrooms, wiped clean
45 cl/³/4 pint	unsalted vegetable stock
2 tbsp	cornflour
2 tbsp	thick Greek yogurt
¹/4 tsp	salt
	freshly ground black pepper

Rinse the beans under cold running water, then put them into a large, heavy pan, and pour in enough cold water to cover them by about 7.5 cm (3 inches). Discard any beans that float to the surface. Cover the pan, leaving the lid ajar, and slowly bring the liquid to the boil. Boil the beans for 2 minutes, then turn off the heat and soak the beans, covered, for at least 1 hour. (Alternatively, soak the beans overnight in cold water.)

Rinse the beans, place them in a clean saucepan, and pour in enough water to cover them by about 7.5 cm (3 inches). Bring the liquid to the boil. Boil the beans for 10 minutes, then drain and rinse again. Wash out the pan, replace the beans and pour in enough water to cover them again by about 7.5 cm (3 inches). Add the bay leaves, bring the liquid to the boil, then reduce the heat to maintain a strong simmer, and cook the beans until they are tender—about1 hour. If the beans appear to be drying out at any point, pour in more hot water. Drain the beans, rinse them

and drain them again. Set the beans aside and keep them warm.

Preheat the oven to 170°C (325°F or Mark 3).

Place the wild rice with the cinnamon stick and ¹/2 teaspoon of the salt in a small ovenproof dish. Bring 60 cl (1 pint) of water to the boil and pour it over the rice. Cover the dish with a lid and bake the rice for 1 hour. Drain off all but about 1 tablespoon of water. Leave the rice, covered, in a warm place for 15 minutes, to allow it to absorb the remaining liquid.

Drain the basmati rice and place it in a large saucepan with the mace and the remaining ¹/2 teaspoon of salt. Add 3 litres (5 pints) of water and bring it to the boil. Reduce the heat to low, cover the pan and simmer the rice for 20 minutes, or until tender. When the rice is cooked, drain it, cover and keep warm.

While the basmati rice is cooking, prepare the mushroom ragout. Melt the butter in a large heavy bottomed saucepan over medium heat, add the onion and cook it gently for 5 to 6 minutes, until it is softened but not browned. Add the mushrooms and cook for a further 2 to 3 minutes, until they are slightly softened. Pour in the stock and bring it to the boil, then cover the pan and reduce the heat. Simmer for 10 minutes, until the mushrooms are soft. Blend the cornflour with the yogurt and stir it into the mushrooms with the salt and some black pepper. Continue cooking for 3 to 4 minutes, until the sauce thickens slightly. Transfer the ragout to a serving bowl and keep it warm.

Meanwhile, bring about 4cm(1¹/2 inches) of water to the boil with the brown sugar in a large non-reactive saucepan. Add the sweetcorn and bring the water back to the boil, reduce the heat, and simmer, covered, until just tender—about 5 minutes. Drain the sweetcorn in a colander.

Place half the nut oil in a warmed serving bowl. Discard the bay leaves from the beans and the cinnamon stick and blades of mace from the rices. Transfer the beans, rices and sweetcorn to the oiled serving bowl. Pour over the remaining oil, add the nutmeg and some pepper, then toss all the ingredients together. Serve immediately, with the mushroom ragout.

Editor's Note: If wild mushrooms are unavailable, subsb-tute button and chestnut mushrooms. The pilaff is also delicious served cold as a salad, with a little cider vinegar added

Pumpkin and Pecorino Risotto

Serves 4

Working (and total) time: about l hour and l5 minutes

Calories 305, Protein 6g, Cholesterol 5mg, fat 6g,
Saturated fat 2g, Sodium 280mg

1 tbsp	virgin olive oil
2	shallots, finely chopped
250 g/8 oz	Italian round-grain rice
500 g/1 lb	pumpkin, peeled, seeded and finely grated
¹/₄ tsp	powdered saffron
8 cl/3 fl oz	dry white wine
90 cl/1 ¹/₂ pints	unsalted vegetable stock
1 tbsp	finely chopped fresh oregano, or 1 tsp dried oregano
¹/₂ tsp	salt
	freshly ground black pepper
30 g/1 oz	pecorino cheese, finely grated
2 tbsp	finely chopped flat-leaf parsley, for garnish (optional)

Heat the oil in a 2 to 3 litre (3 ¹/₂ to 5 pint) fireproof casserole. Add the shallots and cook them over mediumheat for about 5 minutes, stirring from time to time, until they are soft but not brown. Reduce the heat tolow, add the rice, and stir to ensure that each grain is coated with a little oil. Add the grated pumpkin and stir well over medium heat for about 3 minutes, until it is evenly heated through. Stir the saffron into the white wine. Increase the heat and pour the wine into the casserole. Stir constantly until all the liquid has been absorbed—about 3 minutes Meanwhile, heat the stock in a separate pan.

Reduce tha heat under the rice and ladle in about 15 cl (¹/₄ pint) of hot stock into the casserole. Stir well, then place the lid on the casserole to almost cover the top. Simmer gently until all the stock has been absorbed—about 5 minutes Stir in another ladleful of stock and cover as before This time, stir the contents of the casserole once or twice while the stock is being absorbed, replacing the lid after stirring. Mix in the oregano, then continue to add stock by the ladleful, stirring frequently, until the rice is soft but still a little resilient to the bite, and the pumpkin has almost melted into a sauce—about 30 minutes. Once this stage has been reached, stir in the remaining stock and replace the lid on the casserole. Turn off the heat and leave the risotto to stand for 5 minutes, during which time the remaining stock will be absorbed. Meanwhile, warm four serving bowls

Season the risotto with the salt, some pepper and the pecorino cheese, stirring well until the cheese has melted. Serve immediately, if you like, sprinkle ¹/₂ tablespoon of chopped parsley over each portion.

Pea and Mushroom Risotto

Serves 6

Working time about 45 minutes

Total time about 1 hour and 15 minutes

Calories 410, Protein 12g, Cholesterol 20mg, Total fat
10g, Saturated fat 5g, Sodium 430mg

350 g/12 oz	*peas, shelled or 125 g (4 oz) frozen peas, thawed*
30 g/1 oz	*unsalted butter*
l25g/4 oz	*shallots, chopped*
500g/1 lb	*brown round-grain rice*
20 cl/7 fl oz	*dry white wine or dry vermouth*
45 cl/³/₄ pint	*tomato juice*
45 cl/³/₄ pint	*unsalted vegetable stock*
250 g	*tomatoes, skinned, seeded (page 14) and chopped*
¹/₂ tsp	*salt*
250 g/8 oz	*chestnut mushrooms, wiped clean and coarsely grated*
60 g/2 oz	*Parmesan cheese, grated*
	freshly ground black pepper
	chopped parsley, for garnish

If you are using fresh peas, boil them until barely tender—3 to 4 minutes. Drain them, then refresh them under cold running water. Drain them again and set aside (Frozen peas do not need precooking.)

In a large, heavy-bottomed saucepan, melt the butter and saute the shallots over medium heat until they are transparent, stirring occasionally—3 to 5 minutes. Stir the rice into the shallots and cook it for 2 to 3 minutes, stirring constantly to ensure that the grains are well coated with the butter.

Pour the wine into the rice and simmer, stirring frequently, until the wine has been absorbed by the rice. Pour in the tomato juice and 30 cl (¹/₂ pint) of the stock, bring the liquid to the boil, then reduce the heat to a simmer. Cover the saucepan and cook the rice, stirring occasionally, for about 20 minutes Stir the tomatoes and the salt into the rice, cover and simmer for a further 10 minutes, adding more stock, a ladleful at a time, if the rice dries out.

Add the mushrooms, peas and any remaining stock to the pan, increase the heat to high and cook rapidly, stirring constantly, until the stock is absorbed but the rice is still very moist. Stir the Parmesan cheese into the risotto and season it generously with freshly ground pepper Turn the risotto into a warmed serving dish and sprinkle it with chopped parsley.

Editor's Note:If preferred, 90 cl(1 ¹/₂ pints)of unsalted vegetable stock may be used instead of the combination o tomato juice and stock.

Eight Treasures in Lotus Leaves

Serves 4

Working time: about 1 hour and 30 minutes

Total time about 12 hours (includes soaking)

Calories 553, Protein 19g, Cholesterol 0mg, Total fat 14g, Saturated fat 3g, Sodium 250mg

4	dried lotus leaves, soaked for 30 minutes in hot water, rinsed in cold water and dried carefully on a tea towel
500 g/1 lb	fresh lotus roots, or 90 g (3 oz) dried lotus roots, soaked for 8 hours or overnight in tepid water
45 cl/³/₄ pint	unsalted vegetable stock or water
2 tbsp	rice wine or medium-dry sherry
2 tsp	sugar
¹/₈ tsp	salt
1 25 cm/1¹/₂ inch	piece fresh ginger root, sliced
1	garlic clove
3	spring onions, each cut into three pieces
45 g/1 ¹/₂ oz	canned skimmed whole lotus nuts drained
1 tsp	low-sodium soy sauce or shoyu
4 or 5	fresh coriander sprigs, leaves only for garnish

Rice stuffing

24	fresh chestnuts, peeled or dried chestnuts, soaked for at least-8 hours or overnight in hot water and drained
60 g/2 oz	mung beans, soaked for 1 to 2 hours
60 g/2 oz	adzuki beans, soaked for 1 to 2 hours in water
12	dried shiitake mushrooms, soaked for 20 minutes in hot water
250 g/8 oz	long-grain rice
1 tsp	safflower oil
1 or 2	garlic cloves, finely chopped
¹/₂ tbsp	grated fresh ginger root
175g/6 oz	bamboo shoots, finely diced
2	carrots, diced
3	spring onions, white and green parts separated and diced
90 g/3 oz	roasted unsalted peanuts
¹/₄ tsp	sugar
¹/₄ tsp	salt
1 tsp	low-sodium soy sauce or shoyu

First prepare the rice stuffing. Simmer the chestnuts in water to cover for 20 to 25 minutes, until just tender. Bring the water to the boil and continue to boil until nearly all the liquid has evaporated, turning the chestnuts several times.

Drain the mung and adzuki beans, rinse them and drain them again. Simmer the two sorts of bean sepa rately in fresh water to cover until tender—about 10 minutes for the mung beans, and up to 25 minutes for the adzuki beans—skimming several times during cooking. Drain and rinse the beans, reserving the liquid from the adzuki beans.

Drain the mushrooms, and strain and reserve their soaking liquid. Dice the mushrooms, discarding the stalks, and set them aside.

Rinse the rice several times in cold water. Mix the adzuki bean liquid with the mushroom-soaking liquid and make it up to ¹/₂ litre(16 fl oz)with water. Put this in a large saucepan with the rice and bring to a fast boil, then cook the rice, uncovered, for 10 to 15 minutes, until most of the liquid has evaporated. Cover the pan tightly, reduce the heat to the lowest setting possible, and cook very gently for a further 10 minutes. Turn off the heat and leave the rice to steam, covered, for about 10 minutes. Remove the lid, fluff up the rice with a pair of chopsticks and leave to cool. (The rice will be tinted pale pink from the adzuki bean liquid.)

Heat a wok or large, heavy frying pan until very hot. Add the oil and drop in the garlic and ginger to sizzle and become aromatic, then add the mushrooms, bamboo shoots, carrots, chestnuts and white parts of the spring onions at 10 to 12 second intervals, tossing and stirring all the time with a wok scoop or spatula. Transfer the contents of the pan to a large bowl, add the rice, the green parts of the spring onions, the peanuts, sugar, salt and soy sauce, and mix well together to complete the stuffing.

Make up four lotus-leaf parcels, each filled with a quarter of the rice stuffing. Steam the parcels in a bamboo or metal steamer over boiling water for 20 to 25 minutes.

Meanwhile, scrub the fresh lotus roots well and cut them diagonally into 5 mm ($1/4$ inch) slices. (If you are using reconstituted dried lotus roots, rinse them thoroughly before slicing.)

Bring the stock or water to the boil, add the rice wine, sugar, salt, ginger, garlic and spring onions, and return to the boil. Add the whole lotus nuts and sliced roots, and simmer for 35 minutes. Remove the nuts, ginger, garlic and spring onions with a slotted spoon;

reserve the nuts and keep them warm, and discard the ginger, garlic and onions. (If you are using dried roots, simmer them for another 15 minutes.) Add the soy sauce to the cooking liquid, bring to the boil, and reduce it until the sauce becomes syrupy—10 to 12 minutes. Return the nuts to the sauce to heat through

Place a steamed lotus parcel on each of four individual plates and cut a square window in the parcel with scissors. Serve the rice-stuffed parcels with the braised lotus roots and nuts, garnished with coriander leaves.

Editor's Note : All the unusual ingredients called for In this recipe can be obtalned in Chinese grocery shops. SInce most of the ingredients are dried, any unused surplus can be stored almost indefinitely and used on another occasion.

Rice Cakes with Onion Relish

Serves 4

Working time: about 35 minutes

Total time: about 1 hour and 45 minutes (includes soaking)

Calories 255, Protein 8g, Cholesterol 15mg, Total fat 6g, Saturated fat 3g, Sodium 300mg

175 g/6 oz	basmati rice, rinsed under cold running water until the water runs clear, then soaked for 1 hour in 1 litre(1 $3/4$ pints)water
$1/2$ tsp	safflower oil
1	onion, finely chopped
125 g/4 oz	carrots, grated
2	hot green chilli peppers, finely chopped
2	garlic cloves, crushed
2 tsp	cardamom seeds. crushed
1 tbsp	chopped fresh conander
$1/2$ tsp	ground cumin
$1/4$ tsp	qround turmeric
60 g/2 oz	Cheddar cheese, grated
$1/4$ tsp	salt

Onion relish

1	onion, cut into paper-thin rings
$1/2$	sweet red pepper, finely chopped
1	lime, finely grated rind and juice
$1/4$ tsp	salt
$1/2$ tsp	paprika
$1/2$ tsp	brown sugar

First make the onion relish. Place the onion in a bowl with the sweet red pepper, and add the lime rind, lime juice, salt, paprika and sugar. Toss the ingredients to-

gether until well combined, then transfer them to a serving bowl and set them aside for the flavours to develop while you prepare the rice cakes.

Drain the rice and put it in a large saucepan, add 1.5 litres (2 $1/2$ pints) of water and bring to the boil. Boil the rice rapidly, uncovered, until thoroughly tender— about 10 minutes. The rice needs to be well cooked so that the rice cakes will hold together when they are grilled. Drain the rice and set it aside

Heat the oil in a heavy frying pan over medium heat and fry the chopped onion for 3 to 4 minutes, until softened and beginning to brown. Stir in the carrots, chili peppers, garlic, cardamom, coriander, cumin and turmeric, and cook, stirring continuously, until the carrots have softened—about 2 minutes. Remove the pan from the heat, stir in the rice, cheese and salt, and mash the mixture with a potato masher, until the rice is broken up and sticky.

Preheat the grill to medium. Lightly flour your hands and shape the mixture into 20 small balls. Thread five balls on to each of four skewers. Place the skewers on a foil-covered rack and grill the cakes for about 15 minutes, turning once, until they are a pale golden colour. Serve hot, accompanied by the onion relish.

Editor's Note: If you use wooden skewers, soak them in water for about 10 minutes before threading them with the rice balls to prevent them from burning under the grill

Basmati and Wild Rice Moulds with Braised Artichokes

Serves 6

Working time: about 1 hour and 30 minutes

Total time: about 2 hours and 30 minutes (includes soaking)

Calories 405, Protein 14 g, Cholesterol 25 mg, Total fat 12 g, Saturated fat 5 g, Sodium 245 mg

125 g/4 oz	*wild rice*
125 g/4 oz	*basmati rice, rinsed under cold running water until the water runs clear, then soaked in 60 cl (1 pint) water for 1 hour*
1/2 tsp	*salt*
6	*globe artichokes*
2	*lemons, grated rind of one, juice of both*
1 tbsp	*virgin olive oil*
3 tbsp	*chopped mint*
2	*garlic cloves, finely chopped*
125 g/4 oz	*fresh chestnuts, peeled (page 37), or 60 g (2 oz) dried chestnuts, soaked in hot water for 8 hours or overnight*

Pour 1.25 litres (2 pints) of water into a saucepan and bring it to the boil. Stir in the wild rice, reduce the heat and simmer the rice, uncovered, until it is tender but still has bite—about 45 minutes.Meanwhile,drain the basmati rice and place it in a large saucepan with the salt. Add 90 cl (1 1/2 pints) of water, bring it to the boil and boil it rapidly, uncovered, for 5 minutes until the rice is cooked. Drain the basmati rice and set it aside.

While the wild rice is cooking, prepare the artichokes. Put 3 litres (5 pints) of water in a large bowl and add a third of the lemon juice. Break or cut the stem off one of the artichokes. Snap off and discard the outer leaves, starting at the base and continuing until you reach the pale yellow leaves at the core. Cut the top two thirds off the artichoke. Trim away any dark green leaf bases that remain on the artichoke bottom. Cut the artichoke bottom in half and remove the hairy choke and all the pinkish central leaves. Then cut each half into six wedges. Drop the wedges into the acidulated water until required. Repeat these steps to prepare the remaining artichokes.

Heat the oil in a large heavy frying pan over medium heat. Add the mint and garlic and cook for about 1 minute. Drain the artichokes, add them to the pan and stir-fry them for 1 minute. Add the remaining lemon juice and 1/4 litre (8 fl oz) of water, cover and simmer for about 10 minutes. Remove the lid and cook for a further 5 to 10 minutes, until the artichokes are tender.

A few minutes before the end of cooking the artichokes, prepare the rice moulds. Drain the wild rice.Chop the chestnuts finely Melt the butter in a pan add the chestnuts and fry them for 2 to 3 minutes. Add the basmati and wild rice. Mix them well and heat through. Divide the rice mixture among six 20 cl (7 fl oz) moulds or cups and carefully turn each one out on to a hot individual serving plate.

Arrange the artichoke wedges alongside the rice. Stir the lemon rind and some white pepper into the juices left in the pan and spoon the mixture over the artichokes. Serve immediately.

Gateau of Crepes with Wild Rice and Mushrooms

Serves 6

Working time: about 1 hour

Total time: about 2 hours

Calories 215, Protein 8 g, Cholesterol 40 mg, Total fat 7 g, Saturated fat 2 g, Sodium 185mg

125 g/4 oz	*plain flour*
1 tsp	*freshly grated nutmeg*
1	*small egg*
1	*egg white*
30 cl/1/2 pint	*skimmed milk*
60 g/2 oz	*wild rice*
30 g/1 oz	*dried ceps or other wild mushrooms*
1 1/2 tbsp	*dry Madeira*
1 1/2 tbsp	*safflower oil*
250 g/8 oz	*button mushrooms, wiped clean. thinly sliced*
1/2 tsp	*salt*
60 g/2 oz	*low-fat fromage frais*
	freshly ground black pepper

First make the batter for the crepes. Sift the flour into

a bowl and mix in the nutmeg. Make a well in the centre and add the egg, egg white and a little of the milk Beat the eggs and milk, gradually working in the dry ingredients; as the batter thickens, add the rest of the milk in several stages to make a smooth batter. Cover the bowl and let the batter stand for 1 hour.

Bring 30 cl (1/2 pint) of water to the boil in a saucepan. Stir in the wild rice, reduce the heat and simmer, uncovered, until the rice is tender but still has bite— approximately 45 minutes, then drain.

Meanwhile, put the ceps in a small bowl and add 1 tablespoon of the Madeira and 60 cl (1 pint) of tepid water to cover them. Set the mushrooms aside to soak for 20 to 30 minutes.

When the batter has rested, heat a 20 cm (8 inch) crepe pan or non-stick frying pan over medium heat. Add 1/4 teaspoon of the oil and spread it over the entire surface with a paper towel. Continue heating the pan until it is very hot and the oil is almost smoking. Put about 3 tablespoons of the batter into the hot pan and immediately swirl the pan to coat the bottom with a thin, even layer of batter. Pour any excess batter back into the bowl. Cook the crepe until the bottom is browned—about 1 minute. Lift the edge with a spatula and turn the crepe over. Cook the crepe on the second side until it, too, is browned—15 to 30 seconds. Slide the crepe on to a plate. Repeat the process with the remaining batter to make six crepes in all, brushing the pan lightly with more oil if the crepes begin to stick, and stacking the cooked crepes on the plate as

you go. Cover the crepes with a towel to prevent them from drying out, and set them aside.

Preheat the oven to 180°C (350°F or Mark 4).

Drain and rinse the ceps and strain their soaking liquid through muslin or a coffee filter paper; reserve the liquid. Heat the remaining oil in a heavy-bottomed saucepan . Add the button mushrooms and saute them for about 3 to 5 minutes, until lightly cooked. Add the ceps, the reserved soaking liquid, the salt and the remaining 1/2 tablespoon of Madeira. Bring the liquid to the boil and boil it fast for 30 seconds. Reduce the heat, stir in the wild rice and cook over medium heat for about 2 minutes, to heat the rice through . Drain the rice and mushrooms, reserving the liquid. Return the mixture to the pan, season it with some black pepper, then cover it and keep it warm.

Pour the reserved liquid into a small saucepan and boil hard over high heat to reduce it to about 3 tablespoons. Take the pan off the heat and stir in the fromage frais. Reduce the heat to low, then gently warm the sauce; do not allow it to boil. Cover and keep warm while you make the gateau.

Place one crepe on a large ovenproof plate. Spoon one fifth of the rice and mushroom mixture evenly over the crepe, then cover the mixture with another crepe and continue alternating layers of rice and mushroom mixture with crepes to make a gateau. Place the crepe gateau in the oven for a few minutes to warm it through. Serve the gateau at once, cut into wedges and accompanied by the sauce.

Red Lentils with White Rice and Pearl Onions

Serves 6 as a side dish

Working time: about 15 minutes

Total time: about 30 minutes

Calories 200, Protein 8g, Cholesterol 0mg, Total fat 3g, Saturated fat 0g, Sodium 20mg

90 g/6 ¹/₂ oz	*red lentils, picked over*
90 g/3 oz	*long-grain rice*
2 tbsp	*sugar*
4 tbsp	*raspberry vinegar*
6 tbsp	*unsalted chicken stock*
175 g/6 oz	*pearl onions, blanched for 2 minutes in boiling water and peeled*
1 tsp	*Dijon mustard*
	freshly ground black pepper
1 tbsp	*safflower oil*

Bring the lentils and ³/₄ litre (1¹/₄ pints) of water to the boil in a small saucepan over medium-high heat. Reduce the heat and simmer the lentils until they are tender—15 to 20 minutes. Avoid overcooking or the lentils will lose much of their colour. Drain the lentils and put them into a large bowl.

Start cooking the rice while the lentils are simmering. Bring the rice and ¹/₄ litre (8 fl oz) of water to the boil in a small saucepan over medium-high heat. Reduce the heat, cover the saucepan, and sirhmer the rice until the liquid has been absorbed and the rice is tender—about 20 minutes. Add the rice to the lentils.

While the rice is cooking, sprinkle the sugar into a saute pan and set it over medium heat. Cook the sugar until it liquefies and starts to caramelize. Pour in 3 tablespoons of the vinegar and 4 tablespoons of the chicken stock. As the liquid comes to a simmer, stir it to incorporate the caramelized sugar, then add the pearl onions. Cook the onions, stirring from time to time, until they are glazed and nearly all the liquid in the pan has evaporated. Add the glazed onions to the lentils and rice in the bowl.

To prepare the dressing, combine the remaining raspberry vinegar and chicken stock, the mustard and some pepper in a small bowl. Whisk in the oil, then pour the vinaigrette over the lentil and rice mixture, and toss well. This salad is best served cold.

Black Bean, Rice and Pepper Salad

Serves 4 as a main course

Working time: about 20 minutes

Total time: about 11 hours (includes soaking and chilling)

Calories 635, Protein 21 g, Cholesterol 2 mg, Total fat 10 g, Saturated fat 1 g, Sodium 385 mg

185 g/6 ¹/₂ oz	*black beans, picked over, soaked for 8 hours (or over night and drained*
1	*small onion, coarsely chopped*
1	*gariic clove*
2 tsp	*fresh thyme, or ¹/₂ tsp dried thyme leaves*
1	*bayleaf*
¹/₂ tsp	*salt*
1 litre/1³/₄ pints	*unsalted chicken stock*
370 g/13 oz	*long-grain rice*
2	*shallots, finely chopped*
1	*sweet red pepper, seeded. deribbed and sliced into short, thin strips*
1	*sweet green pepper, seeded, deribbed and sliced into short, thin strips*
1	*fresh hot green chili pepper, seeded.and finely chopped*
3	*spring onions, trimmed and thinly sliced*
2 tbsp	*chopped fresh coriander or parsley*
Chili dressing	
1 tsp	*Dijon mustard*
1 tbsp	*sherry vinegar or white wine vinegar*
1 tbsp	*unsalted chicken stock*
2 tbsp	*virgin olive oil*
1/2 tsp	*chillipowder*
4	*drops Tabasco sauce*
1	*garlic clove, finely chopped*
	freshly ground black pepper

Put the beans into a large, heavy-bottomed saucepan, and pour in enough cold water to cover them by about

7.5 cm (3 inches). Bring the water to the boil. Boil the beans for 10 minutes, then drain.

Return the beans to the pan, add enough water to cover them by 7.5 cm (3 inches) and bring to the boil. Add the onion, garlic, thyme and bay leaf to the beans, tightly cover the pan and simmer the beans, occasionally skimming foam from the surface of the liquid, until they are soft—about 50 minutes. Stir in the salt and continue cooking the beans until they are quite tender—30 minutes to 1 hour more. If the beans appear to be drying out at any point, pour in more water.

Transfer the cooked beans to a colander. Remove the garlic clove and bay leaf, then rinse the beans and drain them well.

Bring the stock to the boil in a small saucepan. Add the rice and shallots, and lower the heat to maintain a simmer. Cook the rice, covered, until it is tender and the liquid is absorbed—about 20 minutes.

While the rice is cooking, prepare the dressing Combine the mustard, vinegar and the tablespoon of stock in a small bowl. Whisk in the oil, then the chilli powder, Tabasco sauce, garlic and some pepper.

Transfer the hot rice to a large bowl Add the peppers, spring onions and beans. Pour the dressing over the salad, toss well, and chill the salad for at least 1 hour. Sprinkle the salad with the fresh coriander o parsley just before serving.

Editor's Note: Instead of soaking the beans overnight, they can be put in a pan with enough cold water to cover by 5 cm (3 inches), boiled for 2 minutes, then left to soak (off the heat and covered) for at least 1 hour, and drained.

Saffron Rice Salad with Peppers and Chick-Peas

Serves 12 as a side dish

Working lime: about 30 minutes
Total time: about 2 hours and 45 minutes
Calories 180, Protein 5 g, Cholesterol 0 mg Total fat 7 g,
Saturated fat 1 g, Sodium 145 mg

135 g/4¹/₂ oz	dried chick-peas picked over
¹/₄ tsp	salt
275 g/9 oz	long-grain rice
60 cl/1 pint	unsalted chicken stock or water
¹/₂ tsp	saffron threads, soaked for 10 minutes in very hot water
1	strip lemon rind
500 g/1 lb	fresh peas, shelled, or 150 g (5 oz) frozen peas, thawed
30 g/1 oz	whole unskinned almonds
1	sweet red pepper, seeded, deribbed and cut into thin slices
1	sweet green pepper, seeded, deribbed and cut into thin slices
2	ripe tomatoes, seeded and chopped
6	oil-cured black olives, thinly sliced
6 tbsp	vinaigrette

Rinse the chick-peas under cold running water. Put the chick-peas in a large, heavy pan and pour in enough cold water to cover them by about 5 cm (2 inches). Discard any chick-peas that float to the surface. Cover the pan, leaving the lid ajar, and bring the water to the boil; cook for 2 minutes Turn off the heat, cover the pan, and soak the peas for at least 1 hour. (Alternatively, soak the chick-peas overnight in cold water.)

When the chick-peas finish soaking, drain them well in a colander. Return them to the pan and pour in enough water to cover them by about 5 cm (2 inches). Bring the liquid to a simmer; cook the chick-peas over medium-low heat until they are soft—about 45 minutes. Stir in the salt and continue cooking the chick-peas until they are quite tender—10 to 15 minutes more. (If the chick-peas appear to be drying out at any point, pour in more water.)

About 20 minutes before the chick-peas finish cooking, start the rice: bring the stock or water to the boil in a saucepan, then add the rice, the saffron and its soaking liquid, and the lemon rind. Stir the rice to distribute the saffron and return the liquid to the boil. Cover the pan and cook the rice over medium-low heat until it is tender and has absorbed all the liquid—about 20 minutes. Discard the lemon rind.

While the rice is cooking, boil the fresh peas until they are tender—5 to 7 minutes. (Frozen peas do not require boiling but can be blanched briefly.) Drain the peas and set them aside. Heat the almonds in a small, heavy frying pan over medium heat, stirring frequently until they are lightly toasted—about 5 minutes.

Drain the chick-peas well and transfer them to a large bowl. Add the rice, peas, toasted almonds, red and green peppers, tomatoes and olives. Pour the prepared vinaigrette over the salad and toss the ingredients well to coat them. Transfer the salad to a serving dish. Serve at room temperature or barely chilled.

Brown Rice and Mango Salad

Serves 8 as a side dish
Working time: about 20 minutes
Total time: about 1 hour and 30 minutes
Calories 140, Protein 2g, Cholesterol 0mg, Total fat 4g,
Saturated fat 0g, Sodium 70mg

185 g/6¹/₂ oz	*brown rice*
4 tbsp	*red wine vinegar*
¹/₄ tsp	*salt*
2 tbsp	*safflower oil*
1	*sweet green pepper, seeded and deribbed*
1	*small shallot, finely chopped*
¹/₈ tsp	*ground cardamom*
	mace
	cayenne pepper
1	*ripe mango, peeled and diced*

Bring 1.5 litres (2¹/₂ pints) of water to the boil in a large saucepan. Stir in the rice, reduce the heat and simmer the rice, uncovered, until it is tender—about 35 minutes. Drain the rice and put it in a serving bowl. Stir in the vinegar and salt, and allow the mixture to cool to room temperature—about 30 minutes.

When the rice is cool, stir in the oil, pepper, shallot, cardamom and a pinch each of mace and cayenne pepper. Add the mango pieces and stir them in gently so that they retain their shape. Cover the salad; to allow the flavours to meld, let the salad stand, unrefrigerated, for about 30 minutes before serving it.

Caribbean Spiced Rice

Serves 4

Working (and total) time about 50 minutes

Calories 540, Protein 9g, Cholesterol 0mg, Total fat 6g,
Saturated fat 2g, Sodium 250mg

350 g/12 oz	*basmati rice, rinsed under cold running water until the water runs clear*
1 tsp	*groundall spice*
1/2 tsp	*salt*
2	*garlic cloves, sliced*
	freshly ground black pepper
90 cl/1 1/2 pints	*unsalted vegetable stock*
2	*green bananas*
1 tbsp	*white wine vinegar*
1	*small carrot, finely chopped*
1/4	*sweet red pepper, finely chopped*
1	*stick celery, finely chopped*
125 g/4 oz	*okra, finely sliced*
2	*small ripe mangoes*
12	*spring onions, finely sliced*
6 tbsp	*chopped parsley*
1/2	*fresh lime, cut into slices, for garnish*

Coriander sauce

20 g/3/4 oz	*fresh coriander leaves*
4	*spring onions, roughly chopped*
1	*garlic clove, roughly chopped*
1/2	*onion, roughly chopped*
1 cm/1/2 inch	*piece fresh ginger root, peeled and roughly chopped*
1/2	*green chilli pepper, seeded and roughly chopped*
	freshly ground black pepper
4 tsp	*wine vinegar*
1/2	*fresh lime, juice only*
2 tbsp	*virgin olive oil*

First make the coriander sauce. Put all the ingredients in a blender with 2 tablespoons of water and blend until smooth. Turn the sauce into a small serving bowl, cover it and set it aside.

Put the rice in a saucepan with the, allspice, salt, garlic and some black pepper, and pour in the unsalted vegetable stock. Bring the stock to a simmer, cover the pan and slowly simmer until the rice is cooked and the water absorbed—about 20 minutes.

Meanwhile, cut the bananas in half lengthwise without peeling them. With a sharp knife score the skin through to the flesh in a few places. Put the bananas in a saucepan, pour in enough cold water to cover them and add the vinegar. Bring the liquid to the boil and simmer for 20 minutes. When the bananas are cooked, drain and peel them. Cut each half lengthwise into three or four thin slices. Set the bananas aside and keep them warm.

While the rice and bananas are cooking, steam the vegetables. Pour enough water into a saucepa it 2.5 cm (1 inch) deep. Set a vegetable steamer in the saucepan, and bring the water to the boil. Put the carrot in the steamer and steam it for 3 minutes, then add, the sweet red pepper, the celery and the okra. Steam the vegetables until they are cooked but still firm and crisp—a further 5 to 6 minutes. Set them aside and keep them warm.

Peel the mangoes. Cut off the two cheeks from each mango, slice them thinly and set them aside Dice the remaining flesh and discard the stones.

When the rice is cooked, stir in the diced ma spring onions, steamed vegetables and parsley then turn the mixture into a serving dish. Serve the rice the banana, mango slices and a slice of lime companied by the coriander sauce.

Salad of Avocado, Flageolets, Almonds and Brown Rice

Serves 6

Working time: about 25 minutes

Total time about 3 hours, (includes soaking)

Calories 300, Protein 10g, Cholesterol 0mg, Total fat 11g, Saturated fat 2g, Sodium 80mg

125 g/4 oz	*dried flageolet beans,picked over*
250 g/8 oz	*brown rice*
1/4 tsp	*salt*
1	*small ripe avocado*
1	*lemon, juice only, strained*
60 g/2 oz	*blanched and skinned almonds toasted*
6 tbsp	*chopped parsley*
2 tbsp	*chopped -fresh wild fennel*
4 tbsp	*plain low-fat yogurt*
1 tbsp	*virgin olive oil*
1 tsp.	*Dijon mustard*
	garlic clove crushed
1	*large lettuce, leaves ,washed and dried for garnish*

Rinse the beans under cold running, water, then put them into a large, heavy pan, and pour enough cold water to cover them by about 7.5 cm inches). Discard any beans that float to the surface Cover the pan, leaving the lid ajar, and slowly bring the liquid to the boil. Boil the beans for 2 minutes.then: turn off the heat, and soak the beans, covered.for at least 1 hour. (Alternatively, soak the beans overnight in cold water.)

Rinse the beans, place them in a clean saucepan, and pour in enough water to cover :hem by about 7.5 cm (3 inches). Bring the liquid to the boil Boil the beans for 10 minutes, then dran and rinse again. Wash out the pan, replace the beans and pour in enough water to cover them again by about 7.5 cm (3 inches). Bring the liquid to the boil, then reduce the heat to maintain a strong simmer and cook the beans, covered, until they are tender—about 1 hour If the beans appear to be drying out at any point, pour in more hot water. Drain the beans in a colander, rinse them, and set them aside to cool for about 30 minutes.

Bring 2 litres (3 1/2 pints) of water to the boil in a large saucepan. Stir in the rice and salt, reduce the heat and simmer, uncovered, until the rice is tender—about 40 minutes. Drain the rice in a strainer, rinse under cold water and leave to drain and cool thoroughly.

Halve, stone, peel and chop the avocado and coat the pieces in half of the lemon juice to prevent them from discolouring. In a large bowl, mix the avocado, almonds, parsley and fennel with the beans and rice. In a small bowl, beat together the yogurt, olive oil, mustard, garlic and remaining lemon juice. Fold this dressing into the rice salad.

To serve, line a large bowl with the lettuce leaves and spoon the rice salad into the middle.

Editor's Note: To toast almonds, put them on a baking sheet in a preheated 180°C (350°F or Mark 4) oven for 10 minutes.

Yellow Squash Quiche with a Rice Crust

Serves 4 as a main dish

Working time: about 30 minutes

Total time: about 1 hour and 15 minutes

Calories 320, Protein 17g, Cholesterol 160mg, Total fat 11g, Saturated fat 5g, Sodium 290mg

3 *yellow squashes, halved lengthwise, seeded, flesh grated*
250 g/8 oz *cooked rice*
4 *eggs, whites only of 2*
90 g/3 oz *Emmenthal cheese, grated*
2 tsp *safflower oil*
6 *shallots, finely chopped*
12.5 cl/4 fl oz *vermouth*
¼ tsp *salt*
  freshly ground black pepper
½ tsp *chopped fresh marjoram, or* ¼ tsp *dried marjoram*
½ tsp *fresh thyme, or* ¼ tsp *dried thyme*
¼ litre/8 fl oz *skimmed milk*
⅛ tsp *grated nutmeg*
12 *thin strips of sweet red and green peppers, blanched*

Preheat the oven to 190°C (375°F or Mark 5) To prepare the rice crust, combine the cooked rice, one of the egg whites and half of the cheese. Press the mixture into a 23 cm (9 inch) quiche or flan tin. Prebake the crust until the cheese is just melted—3 to 4 minutes. Remove the crust from the oven and set aside.

Heat the oil in a heavy frying pan over medium heat. Cook the shallots until soft—about 2 to 3 minutes — stirring occasionally. Pour the vermouth into the pan, and cook until the vermouth has nearly evaporated—about 3 minutes. Add the squash and cook, stirring occasionally, until the squash is tender —about 3 minutes. Season the mixture with the salt, pepper, marjoram and thyme, and remove from the heat.

In a large mixing bowl, lightly beat the two whole eggs, the remaining egg white, the skimmed milk and nutmeg. Stir in the remaining cheese and the squash mixture. Pour this mixture into the crust and bake until the filling begins to set—about 20 minutes. Remove the quiche from the oven and arrange the pepper strips on top. Return the quiche to the oven and bake until the filling is set in the centre—5 to 7 minutes more. Cut the quiche into wedges and serve.

Sweet Peppers with Herbed Rice

Serves 8

Working time: about 30 minutes

Total time: about 1 hour and 15 minutes

Calories 235, Protein 4g, Cholesterol 0mg, Total fat 5g, Saturated fat 1g, Sodium 15mg

6	red, yellow or green peppers, grilled and peeled (above)
175 g/6 oz	long-grain brown rice
1	5 cm (2 inch) strip of lemon peel
2 tbsp	virgin olive oil
1	onion, chopped
90 g/3 oz	raisins, soaked in 125 cl(4 fl oz) dry white wine
6 cl/2 fl oz	unsalted chicken or vegetable stock
1	lemon, juice only
3 tbsp	chopped parsley
1 tsp	fresh thyme, or 1/4 tsp dried thyme
1/8 tsp	ground coriander

Bring 1 litre (1³/4 pints) of water to the boil in a saucepan. Add the rice and the lemon peel. Simmer for 25 minutes over medium heat.

Remove the stems, ribs and seeds from the peeled peppers. Cut the peppers in half lengthwise. Set eight of the pepper halves aside as a garnish. Coarsely chop the remaining pepper halves and set them aside too. Preheat the oven to 200°C (400°F or Mark 6).

Heat 1 tablespoon of the oil in a large, heavy frying pan. Add the onion, and cook until it is translucent—about 5 minutes. Add the raisins and wine, stock, and lemon juice. Bring to the boil and add the rice. Stir in the parsley, thyme, coriander and the chopped peppers. Transfer the rice mixture to a 1.5 litre (2¹/2 pint) gratin dish. Mound up the rice slightly and arrange the pepper halves on top. Bake the dish for 20 minutes. Brush the peppers with the remaining oil before serving.

Artichoke Bottoms with Tomato and Rice

Serves 8

Working time: about 25 minutes

Total time: about 45 minutes

Calories 205, Protein 6g, Cholesterol 15mg, Total fat 9g, Saturated fat 4g, Sodium 190mg

4	artichoke bottoms (page 13)
1/2	lemon
40 g/1¹/4 oz	unsalted butter
2 tbsp	virgin olive oil
125 g/4 oz	mushrooms, wiped clean and sliced
1/4 tsp	salt
1	small onion, finely chopped
1	garlic clove, finely chopped
2 tsp	chopped fresh basil, or ³/4 tsp dried basil
2	tomatoes, skinned, seeded and chopped
1/2 litre/16 fl oz	unsalted chicken or vegetable stock
175 g/6 oz	rice
	freshly ground black pepper
60 g/2 oz	Parmesan cheese, freshly grated
10 g/¹/3 oz	parsley, chopped

In a large, non-reactive saucepan, bring 1 litre (1³/4 pints) of water to the boil. Squeeze the juice of the lemon into the water and add the lemon itself. Cook the artichoke bottoms in the boiling water for 10 minutes. Drain them and cut each into six wedges.

In a small, heavy-bottomed saucepan, heat 15 g (¹/2 oz) of the butter with the olive oil over medium heat. Add the mushrooms and salt, and saute until the liquid from the mushrooms has evaporated. Stir in the onion and continue cooking for 2 minutes, stirring frequently. Add the chopped garlic, basil and tomatoes, and 12.5 cl (4 fl oz) of the stock. Bring the mixture to the boil, then reduce the heat and simmer for 10 minutes. Remove the saucepan from the heat.

In a heavy, 4 litre (7 pint) saucepan or a fireproof casserole with a lid, melt the remaining butter over medium-low heat. Add the rice and cook, stirring constantly, until the rice is opaque—3 to 4 minutes. Stir in the vegetable mixture, 1/4 litre (8 fl oz) of the stock and the pepper, and bring to the boil. Reduce the heat and simmer, covered, for 10 minutes.

Gently stir in the artichoke bottoms, the remaining stock and the Parmesan cheese, and continue to cook the dish, covered, until the rice is tender and the liquid is absorbed—10 to 15 minutes.

Garnish with the parsley; serve immediately.

Risotto with Carrots and Coriander

Serves 6

Working (and total) time: about 1 hour

Calories 300, Protein 5g, Cholesterol 30mg, Total fat 11 g,
Saturated fat 6g, Sodium 155mg

45 g/1 ¹/₂ oz	*unsalted butter*
1	*onion, finely chopped*
1 litre/1 ¹/₄ pints	*unsalted chicken stock*
2 tsp	*ground coriander*
300 g/10 oz	*carrots, peeled and finely diced*
350 g/12 oz	*Italian round -grain rice*
	freshly ground black pepper
45 g/1 ¹/₂ oz	*Parmesan cheese, freshly grated*
1	*small bunch fresh coriander leaves, finely chopped*

In a large, heavy-bottomed pan, heat 30g(1 oz) of the butter, and sauté the onion until it is transparent—3 to 5 minutes. Meanwhile, bring the stock to the boil in a saucepan, stir in the ground coriander, reduce the heat and keep the liquid simmering gently.

Add the diced carrots to the onion, and saute them for about 5 minutes. Add the rice, and stir well to ensure that the grains are coated with butter.

Ladle a few spoonfuls of the hot chicken stock into the rice, stir well, and let the mixture cook, stirring occasionally, until most of the liquid has been absorbed by the rice Continue adding hot stock, a little at a time, stirring the mixture constantly and replenishing the liquid as the rice absorbs it. Cook the rice until it is moist but not swimming in the stock, and the grains have lost their brittleness but still retain a chewy core—about 20 minutes.

Remove the rice from the heat and add the remaining butter, the Parmesan cheese and some pepper. Stir the mixture well, cover the pan, and let the risotto stand for 5 minutes. Stir the rice once more, and sprinkle it with the coriander before serving.

Vine Leaves with a Rice and Date Stuffing

Serves 4

Working time: about 35 minutes

Total time about 1 hour

Calories 170, Protein 5g, Cholesterol 0mg, Total fat 2g, Saturated fat 0g, Sodium 90mg

90 g/3 oz	*round-grain brown rice*
125 g/4 oz	*fresh dates, stoned and chopped*
1 tbsp	*pine-nuts, tossed in a frying pan over medium heat until golden, coarsely chopped*
1	*lemon, grated rind and juice of one half, the remainder halved vertically and thinly sliced*
	freshly ground black pepper
8	*large fresh vine leaves, blanched for a few seconds in boiling water, patted dry*

Tomato sauce

1	*small onion, chopped*
250 g/8 oz	*ripe tomatoes, skinned, seeded and chopped*
15cl/¹/₄ pint	*tomato juice*
6 tbsp	*unsalted chicken stock or water*
¹/₈ tsp	*sugar*
1	*bayleaf*
1	*fresh thyme sprig*
	freshly ground black pepper

Bring ¹/₂ litre (16 fl oz) of water to the boil in a saucepan Boil the rice until it is tender—25 to 30 minutes. Drain it thoroughly in a colander.

Meanwhile, place all the sauce ingredients in a small saucepan. Bring the mixture to the boil, cover the pan and simmer over low heat for 15 minutes. Remove the bay leaf and the thyme sprig and purée the sauce in a food processor or blender until it achieves a smooth consistency. (For an even smoother texture, rub the purée through a sieve as well.) Preheat the oven to 190°C (375°F or Mark 5).

Put the rice in a bowl and stir in the dates, pine-nuts, lemon rind and juice, parsley and some pepper. Lay the vine leaves flat on the work surface Place a spoonful of the rice mixture in the centre of each leaf. Fold the stem end up over the filling, fold both sides towards the middle, then roll into a small, tight parcel Lay the parcels on a sheet of foil and wrap them tightly Bake until heated through—about 15 minutes.

Just before serving, reheat the sauce over gentle heat Serve the parcels accompanied by a pool of the sauce and one or two lemon slices.

Editor's Note: Preserved vine leaves may be used if fresh leaves are not available. Wash them In cold water to rid them of excess salt, then drain them thoroughly on a folded tea towel Preserved vine leaves can be tougher than fresh ones after stuffing them, bake them for about 30 minutes.

Spring Onion and Rice Muffins

Makes 12 muffins
Working time: about 20 minutes
Total time: about 45 minutes
Per muffin: Calories 105, Protein 3g, Cholesterol 25mg,
Total fat 3g, Saturated fat 1g, Sodium 130mg

45 g/1 ¹/₂ oz	*long-grain rice*
225 g/7¹/₂ oz	*plain flour*
2 tsp	*baking powder*
2 tsp	*caster sugar*
¹/₄ tsp	*salt*
¹/₄ tsp	*ground white pepper*
1	*egg*
17.5 cl/6 fl oz	*semi-skimmed milk*
2 tbsp	*safflower oil*
2	*spring onions, trimmed and finely chopped*

Preheat the oven to 220°C (425°F or Mark 7). Lightly oil a muffin or deep bun tin Bring 15 cl (¹/₄ pint) of water to the boil in a saucepan. Stir in the rice, then reduce the heat to low, and cover tightly. Cook the rice until it is tender and all the liquid has been absorbed—15 to 20 minutes. Uncover and set aside to cool.

Sift the flour, baking powder, sugar, salt and pepper into a bowl. In another bowl, lightly beat the egg, then whisk in the milk and oil; stir in the cooled rice and the spring onions. Pour the rice mixture into the flour mixture, then stir until the ingredients are just blended.

Spoon the batter into the cups in the tin, filling each no more than two-thirds full. Bake the muffins until lightly browned—18 to 22 minutes. Remove the muffins from the cups immediately and serve hot.

Green and White Rice Salad

Serves 12 as a side dish
Working time: about 25 minutes
Total time: about 45 minutes
Calories 105, Protein 2g, Cholesterol 0mg, Total fat 5g,
Saturated fat 1g, Sodium 123mg

45 cl/³/₄ pint	*unsalted vegetable stock*
175 g/6 oz	*long-grain rice*
400 g/14 oz	*fresh peas, shelled, or 125 g(4 oz)frozen peas, thawed*
¹/₂	*cucumber, cut into 5 mm(¹/₄ inch) dice*
125 g/4 oz	*courgettes, trimmed and jullenned*
6	*spring onions, trimmed and thinly sliced diagonally*
1 tbsp	*finely cut chives*
3 tbsp	*chopped parsley*
1	*crisp round lettuce, leaves washed and dried*

Tarragon vinaigrette

¹/₂ tsp	*French mustard*
¹/₈ tsp	*salt*
¹/₈ tsp	*freshly ground black pepper*
2 tbsp	*tarragon vinegar*
4 tbsp	*walnut or vlrgin olive oil*

Bring the stock to the boil in a small pan and add the rice. Reduce the heat to a simmer and cook the rice, covered, until it is just tender and all the stock is absorbed—15 to 20 minutes. Set aside to cool.

Blanch the fresh peas in a saucepan of boiling water for about 30 seconds; if you are using frozen peas, addthemtoboilingwaterand justbringthewaterback to the boil. Drain the peas, refresh them under cold running water and drain them again.

Transfer the cooled rice to a large bowl, add the blanched peas, the cucumber and courgettes, and mix the ingredients together well. Stir in the spring onion slices, the chives and the parsley.

To make the dressing, whisk the mustard, salt, black pepper, vinegar and oil together in a small bowl. Pour the dressing over the salad, and toss it thoroughly. Place the dressed salad in a rigid plastic container to take to the picnic, and chill it in the refrigerator until you are ready to leave. Place the lettuce leaves in a plastic bag and chill them too.

At the picnic site, line a large serving bowl with the lettuce leaves and pile the salad in the centre.

Sweet Pepper Rice Ring

Serves 6
Working time: about 30 minutes
Total time: about I hour
Calories 125, Protein 3g, Cholesterol 0mg, Total fat 3g,
Saturated fat 1g, Sodium 135mg

¹/₂ tsp	*salt*
150 g/5 oz	*long-grain rice*
1	*small sweet red pepper*
1	*small sweet green pepper*
1	*small sweet yellow pepper*
1 tbsp	*virgin olive oil*
1 tbsp	*white wine vinegar*
1	*garlic clove, crushed*
4 tbsp	*finely chopped parsley*
	freshly ground black pepper
	red, green and yellow pepper rings,for garnish

Bring a saucepan of water to the boil with ¹/₄ teaspoon of the salt. Add the rice, stir it once, then cover the pan and reduce the heat to low. Simmer the rice for 20 minutes, until it is cooked but still slightly firm. Drain it thoroughly and set it aside to cool.

Meanwhile, skin the peppers, then seed and derib them, retaining their juice. Cut the peppers into small dice.

Put the oil, vinegar, garlic and parsley into a large bowl, and add the remaining salt and some pepper. Mix the ingredients well. Add the diced peppers to the dressing, with 1 tablespoon of their juice, then add the rice and mix everything together thoroughly.

Mushroom Risotto

Serves 8

Working (and total) time: about 1 hour and 20 minutes

Calories 285, Protein 7g, Cholesterol 20mg, Total fat 8g, Saturated fat 4g, Sodium 100mg

60 g/2 oz	*dried mushrooms*
45 g/1¹/₂ oz	*unsalted butter*
1	*onion, finely chopped*
1 litre/1³/₄ pints	*unsalted chicken stock*
400g/14 oz	*round-grain brown rice*
4 tbsp	*white wine*
45g/1¹/₂ oz	*freshly grated Parmesan cheese*
2 tbsp	*chopped parsley*
	freshly ground black pepper

Soak the dried mushrooms in warm water for 5 minutes to remove grit Drain them in a colander and soak them again in 60 cl (1 pint) of warm water until they are soft—10 to 15 minutes. Strain off and reserve their second soaking liquid.

In a large, heavy-bottomed saucepan, heat 30g (1 oz) of the butter and saute the onion until it is transparent—3 to 5 minutes. Meanwhile, bring the chicken stock to the boil in a second pan, add the soaking water from the mushrooms, and simmer the liquid over low heat.

Chop the mushrooms roughly and add them to the onions in the pan. Stir the rice into the onion and mushroom mixture and cook it over a gentle heat for about 5 minutes, stirring constantly, to ensure that the grains are well coated with the butter.

Pour the wine into the rice, then begin adding the hot stock, 2 or 3 ladlefuls at a time, stirring frequently. When one batch of liquid has almost been absorbed by the rice, add another few ladlefuls and continue to stir. Cook the rice until it is moist but not swimming in stock, and the grains are no longer brittle but still retain a chewy core—25 to 30 minutes.

Remove the rice from the heat and stir in the remaining butter, the Parmesan cheese, 1 tablespoon of the parsley and some pepper. Cover the pan and leave the risotto to rest for 5 minutes before serving it in soup plates, sprinkled with the remaining parsley.

Gingered Black Beans with Saffron Rice

Serves 6

Working time: about 35 minutes

Total time: about 2 hours and 45 minutes (includes soaking)

Calories 390, Protein 12 g, Cholesterol 0mg, Total fat 14g, Saturated fat 2 g, Sodium 150 mg

175 g/6 oz	*dried black kidney beans, picked over*
2 tbsp	*virgin olive oil*
7.5 cm/3 inch	*piece fresh ginger root, peeled,5 cm (2 inches) thinly sliced, the remainder gra ted*
1 tbsp	*chopped fresh oregano, or 1 tsp dried oregano*
1 tsp	*chopped fresh sage, or ¼ tsp dried sage*
1 tsp	*saffron threads*
½ tsp	*salt*
250 g/8 oz	*long-grain white rice*
90 g/3 oz	*shelled walnuts, roughly chopped*
3	*garlic cloves, crushed*
60 g/2 oz	*dried cloud-ear mushrooms,soaked for 20 minutes in hot water and drained*
125 g/4 oz	*button mushrooms, wiped and sliced*
2	*limes, grated rind and juice*
	freshly ground black pepper
¼ tsp	*paprika, for garnish*

Rinse the beans under cold running water, then put them into a large, heavy pan and pour in enough cold water to cover them by about 7.5 cm (3 inches). Discard any beans that float to the surface. Cover the pan, leaving the lid ajar, and slowly bring the liquid to the boil. Boil the beans for 2 minutes, then turn off the heat and soak the beans, covered, for at least 1 hour.

(Alternatively, soak the beans overnight in cold water.) Rinse the beans, place them in a clean saucepan, and pour in enough water to cover them again by about 7.5 cm (3 inches). Bring the liquid to the boil. Boil the beans for 10 minutes, then drain and rinse again.

In a large, clean saucepan, heat 1 tablespoon of the oil over medium heat; add the sliced ginger root, the oregano and sage, and saute them for 1 minute. Add the beans and enough cold water to cover them by 7.5 cm (3 inches). Bring to the boil, reduce the heat to maintain a strong simmer, and cook the beans until tender—about 1 hou r. Drain them, return them to the pan with all the flavourings and keep them warm.

Bring 60 cl (1 pint) of water to the boil in a saucepan. Add the saffron, salt and rice, and stir once. Cover the pan and simmer for about 15 minutes, or until the rice is just cooked and the water is absorbed. Remove the pan from the heat and stir in the walnuts. Cover the pan again and leave it to stand for a few minutes while the walnuts warm through.

Meanwhile, heat the remaining oil in a wok or large, heavy frying pan over medium heat, then add the garlic, cloud-ear and button mushrooms and the grated ginger. Increase the heat to high and stir-fry them for 5 to 6 minutes, until soft. Add them to the beans, with the lime rind and juice and some pepper.

Pile up the bean mixture in the centre of a large platter and arrange the rice round it. Sprinkle the rice with the paprika and serve at once.

Rice Pudding with Raspberry Sauce

Serves 8

Working time: about 50 minutes

Total time: about 3 hours

Calories 225, Protein 7g, Cholesterol 45mg, Total fat 3 g, Saturated fat 2g, Sodium 140mg

1 litre/1³/₄ pints *semi-skimmed milk*
90 g/3 oz *long-grain rice*
125 g/4 oz *sugar*
¹/₄ tsp *salt*
1 *egg yolk*
3 tbsp *plain flour*
1/2 tsp *grated nutmeg*
1 tsp *pure vanilla extract*
1/4 tsp *almond extract*
45 g/1 ¹/₂ oz *sultanas*
250 g/8 oz *fresh or frozen whole raspberries, thawed*
fresh mint leaves (optional)

Bring ³/₄ litre (1 ¹/₄ pints) of the milk to the boil in a heavy-bottomed saucepan over medium heat. Reduce the heat to low and add the rice, 50 g (1 ¹/₂ oz) of the sugar and the salt. Cook the mixture, stirring frequently, for 50 minutes.

To prepare the pastry cream, whisk together the egg yolk and 4 tablespoons of the remaining milk Whisk in the flour and 50 g (1 ¹/₂ oz) of the remaining sugar; then blend in the remaining milk. Bring the mixture to the boil over medium heat, stirring constantly, then cook it, still stirring vigorously, for 2 minutes more. Remove the pan from the heat and stir in the nutmeg, and vanilla and almond extracts

When the rice has finished cooking, stir in the sultanas, then fold in the pastry cream Transfer the pudding to a clean bowl. To prevent a skin from forming on its surface, press a sheet of plastic film directly on to the pudding. Refrigerate the pudding until it is cold— about 2 hours

To prepare the sauce, purée the raspberries and the remaining 25 g (1 oz) sugar in a blender or food processor. Rub the purée through a fine sieve with a plastic spatula or the back of a wooden spoon, discard the seeds.

To serve, divide the sauce among eight serving dishes. Top the sauce with individual scoops of pudding; if you like, sprinkle the scoops with some additional nutmeg and garnish each with a sprig of mint.

Toasted Brown Rice Cereal with Orange and Cocoa

Serves 6

Working time: about 15 minutes

Total time: about 30 minutes

Calories 215, Protein 3g, Cholesterol 0mg, Total fat 10g, Saturated fat 0g, Sodium 100mg

175 g/6 oz	*brown rice*
1/4 tsp	*salt*
2 tbsp	*unsweetened cocoa powder*
90 g/3 oz	*dark brown sugar*
12 5 cl/4 fl oz	*fresh orange juice*
1	*orange, peeled and cut into segments*

Toast the brown rice in a heavy frying pan over medium-high heat, shaking the pan occasionally, until the rice begins to crackle and some of the kernels start to burst—7 to 10 minutes. Transfer the rice to a blender and grind it until it resembles coarse sand.

Put the ground rice and salt into a saucepan; add ³₄ litre (1 1/4 Pints) of cold water and bring the mixture to a simmer over medium-high heat. Reduce the heat to medium low, then cover the pan and cook the rice until all but about 1/4 litre (8 fl oz) of the water has been absorbed and the rice is tender—approximately 1 minutes. Remove the pan from the heat. Sift the cocoa on to the rice and then stir it in. Add the brown sugar and orange juice; stir the mixture well.

Spoon the cereal into warm bowls, then top each serving with several of the orange segments. Serve the cereal with semi-skimmed milk, if you like.

Rice and Apricot Ring

Serves 8

Working time: about 1 hour and 10 minutes

Total time: about 3 hours and 30 minutes (includes chilling)

Calories 125, Protein 6g, Cholesterol trace, Total fat 1g, Saturated fat trace, Sodium 60mg

60 cl/1 pint	*skimmed milk*
60 g/2 oz	*round-grain rice, washed*
1/2 tsp	*pure almond extract*
5	*large ripe apricots, peeled, halved and stoned, or 400 g (14 oz) canned apricot halves in fruit juice, drained*
90 g/3 oz	*low-fat fromage frais*
1 tbsp	*powdered gelatine*
2	*egg whites*
75 g/2 1/2 oz	*caster sugar*
175 g/6 oz	*fresh raspberries*

ring the milk to the boil in a heavy-bottomed sauce-
an. Reduce the heat to low and add the rice and the
mond extract. Simmer the mixture, uncovered, until
e rice has absorbed all the milk—about 50 minutes—
tirring the mixture from time to time as it cooks.

If you are using fresh apricots, place them, cut side
own, in a non-reactive saucepan and pour in 17.5 cl
fl oz) of boiling water. Simmer the fruit gently for 2
3 minutes, until it is just tender, then drain it.
Arrange eight apricot halves, skinned surfaces down,
the base of a 20 cm (8 inch) ring mould. Reserve the

remaining apricot halves.

When the rice has absorbed the milk, remove it from
the heat and allow it to cool slightly, then stir in the
fromage frais. Dissolve the gelatine in 2 tablespoons
of water (page 13) and stir it into the rice mixture. Whisk
the egg whites until they stand in soft peaks. Whisk in
60 g (2 oz) of the sugar in three batches, ensuring that
the mixture is stiff and glossy each time before adding
further sugar. Stir a spoonful of the egg whites into
the rice to lighten the mixture, then use a metal tablespoon to fold in the remainder of the egg whites. Spoon
the mixture into the prepared ring mould, being care-
ful not to disturb the apricot halves. Level the surface
of the mixture and refrigerate the ring for at least 2
hours, or until set.

Meanwhile, put the raspberries in a non-reactive
saucepan and add the remaining caster sugar. Heat
the berries and sugar gently until the juice runs, then
simmer the berries until they fall apart—2 to 3 minutes. Allow them to cool. Purée the cooked raspberries with the reserved apricot halves in a food processor or blender. Press the purée through a fine nylon
sieve to remove the pips.

To unmould the dessert, dip the base of the mould
in hot water for 2 or 3 seconds, then turn the ring out
on to a flat serving plate. Serve the dessert in slices,
with the raspberry-apricot purée.

Editor's Note: The ring may be stored in the refrigerator for up to four days but it should not be frozen.

Clam and Rice Soup

Serves 4

Working time: about 35 minutes

Total time: about 50 minutes

Calories 140, Protein 7g, Cholesterol 25mg, Total fat 4g, Saturated fat 1g, Sodium 40mg

24	small hard shell clams, scrubbed
1 tbsp	virgin olive oil
90 g/3 oz	onion, finely chopped
2 tsp	finely chopped garlic
1	small bay leaf
45 g/1¹/₂ oz	long-grain rice
4 tbsp	dry white wine
¹/₈ tsp	crushed saffron threads
¹/₂ tsp	fresh lemon juice
1	large, ripe tomato, skinned, seeded and finely chopped
2 tbsp	finely chopped fresh parsley

Bring 1 litre (1³/₄ pints) of water to the boil in a large pan. Add the clams, cover the pan tightly, and cook the clams until they open—about 5 minutes. Transf the clams to a plate, discarding any that remain close and reserve the cooking liquid. When the clams a cool enough to handle, remove them from their shel Discard the shells and set the clams aside.

Heat the oil in a heavy frying pan over medium hea Add the onion, garlic and bay leaf, and saute the stirring frequently, until the onion is translucent— abo 5 minutes.

Strain the clam-cooking liquid through a sieve lin with muslin, then pour the liquid back into the pa Add the contents of the frying pan along with the ric wine, saffron and lemon juice, and bring to the bo Reduce the heat and cover the pan, leaving the lid aj simmer for 10 minutes, stirring once or twice. Add t tomato and simmer for 5 minutes more. Stir in the pa ley and cook for 2 minutes longer. Return the clams the pan and heat them through . Serve immediatel